THE MESSAGE OF THE EAST

"And behold the glory of the God of
Israel came from the way of the East"
—Ezekiel.

"Light shall come again from the East"
—Tyndall.

Vol. I   JANUARY, 1912   No. 1

In the name of the Supreme Being of the
Universe we send out this "Message of the East"
with the hope and prayer that it may bring a
clearer understanding between East and West and
that its spirit may so touch our hearts as to
awaken therein Divine harmony and peace. Un-
charitableness, fanaticism and denunciation do not
belong to the spiritual realm or, indeed, to true
civilization; hence we should strive diligently to
transcend them. God grant that we may be so
genuine and earnest in our spiritual pursuits that
we shall always welcome the message of the Truth
with whole-heartedness, free from bias and preju-
dice, no matter whence that message comes. Truth
is truth whether it comes from the East or the
West. May we with the sword of wisdom, therefore, cut down all the fictitious barriers that divide
race from race, country from country, creed from
creed, and find beneath them the underlying bond
of unity. Then we shall realize that we are members of one universal family, worshipping the same
Supreme Being, and that, as the sages declared in
the Rig Veda: "Truth is one, though men call it
by various names."—EDITOR.

GOD IS EVOLUTION
EVOLUTION IS GOD

GOD IS EVOLUTION
EVOLUTION IS GOD

Essays and Lectures from
MESSAGE OF THE EAST
1912—1961

G_{jw}

Edited by
Gail Northe

VEDANTA CENTRE PUBLISHERS
Cohasset, Mass.

ANANDA ASHRAMA
La Crescenta, CA

Typeset in Goudy and Goudy Handtooled
Design by Rina Dion
Printed by Edwards Brothers
Ann Arbor

$\mathcal{G}_{\jmath_{w}}$

First Edition
Copyright 1993 by
Vedanta Centre, Inc.
All rights reserved.

Published by
Vedanta Centre
130 Beechwood Street
Cohasset, Mass. 02035

Printed in the United States of America.
ISBN 0-911564-40-3

CONTENTS

CONTENTS

FOREWORD

"One single glimpse of Truth stands out like a beacon light." This is the opening sentence of Swami Paramananda's essay "The Eternal Way," and I remember like yesterday such a "glimpse" of Truth. Years later I wrote these lines:

"8 November"

O, that by some fine Mystic
that is Thine
I could express my Joy
—the Joy of long ago
that now again I feel
deep down inside of me.
The Joy
when on this very day
—so long ago that I must stop
and count the years—
so long
and yet it seems like yesterday
when I awoke and said,
"I'm well! I'm well!"

The Cloud of Darkness
that so long had covered me
had
in An Instant
disappeared
and Joy returned!

How can I tell you
what it's like . . .
that deep
black Darkness that encompassed me
for two full years
then
with One Touch
of Mystic Magic
disappeared!

"I'm well!" I said, "I'm well!"
as I awoke that day,
But it was far more
than awaking
from a night of sleep
—or was that really
what it was.

It was in truth
Awaking
from the depths
of my own Self
as would a flower
that had waited long to bloom. . .
—nor was it then

(nor is it yet)
the finest blossom
it could bear.
For two or three or four
more times
the Darkness has returned
so in the depths of me
some growing
could be done.

"It is an awful price to pay
to know yourself,"
a friend once said.
I did not say, but thought—
O no, there is no price
too great to pay for knowing me
—The Me that's really Me—
for this Me is the I—I AM—
that is—the God—the Truth—
in Everyone.

G⌒ⱼ

These lines written in the late 1950's marked my continuing search for higher and higher truths, to become what I knew I was. In the 1985 Fall issue of *Parabola* magazine, I read Marvin

Barrett's review of a book entitled *A Bridge of Dreams—the Story of Paramananda, a Modern Mystic, and His Ideal of All-Conquering Love.* I ordered it immediately. It was not just a story of an Indian Swami who had come to the United States to teach the Vedanta philosophy. It was the story of an illumined soul who fully lived what Christ taught about Love, "Thou shalt love the Lord thy God with all thy heart, and with all thy soul, and with all thy strength and with all thy mind; and thy neighbor as thyself" (Luke 10:27) and who truly obeyed the will of God. "I seek not my own will but the will of the Father which hath sent me" (John 5:30). His words were so simple, so profound, so beautiful and inspiring that I knew without doubt his were the teachings I had been looking for. I soon began acquiring all his published works—over twenty books of essays and lectures, four books of poetry, and all the available volumes of the *Message of the East*, the Vedanta monthly which he founded in 1912 and edited until his passing in 1940. In these volumes I later found one word that I had consistently underlined—*evolution*—"unfold," "evolve," "grow," "blossom," "become"—evolution expressed in different ways.

In 1989, friends at Ananda Ashrama found extra copies of the earliest volumes of the *Message of the East* for the years 1912—1914. In the 1914 edition, I found the answer I had been searching for—the full meaning of the word evolution: not just physical (or organic) evolution, but also moral and spiritual evolution. I learned that the concept of evolution had itself been discovered by one of India's great *rishis*, as they call their ancient men of wisdom. The first discoverer of evolution was Kapila who lived in the 7th century B.C. According to Swami Saradananda, Kapila was one of the "Seven Great *Rishis*" of ancient India, and the founder of the Sankhya philosophy.[1]

The idea of compiling an anthology on moral and spiritual evolution came when I read Swami Saradananda's lecture, "The Problem Universal," which appeared in the 1914 volume of the *Message* and is the lead article of this book. Other essays are by Swami Ramakrishnananda, a disciple of Sri Ramakrishna; Swami Paramananda, and by two of his foremost disciples, Sister Devamata and Sister Daya. All these essays are from the volumes of the *Message*.

The first part of the anthology recalls the great saying of Christ, "Seek ye the kingdom of God"—the kingdom that is within you; the second part, "and all these things shall be added unto you" (Luke 12:31)—love and joy and peace, the fruits of the spirit as St. Paul calls them, which Swami Paramananda so beautifully describes in his wisdom-filled essays.

That is the outline of the anthology, but what would be the title? In November 1991, I read an interview with Dr. Jonas Salk by Bill Moyers. Bill Moyers asked Dr. Salk, "When you use the word evolution do you mean God?" Dr. Salk replied, "If I were to define God I would say God is evolution.

Evolution to me is what God is to others. It's a force that exists, that repels us, that impels us, that causes me to do what I do. It causes you to do what you do."[2]

GOD IS EVOLUTION—EVOLUTION IS GOD

O what a beautiful title! God *is* evolution and evolution *is* God, I thought, because God is everything. "For in him we live and move and have our being" (Acts 17:28).

By God's grace alone this anthology has been realized. It all came from Swami Paramananda. Although I never knew him personally, I am a devotee of his, and I, with deep love and appreciation of his life and work, and gratitude for what he gave to the world, dedicate this volume to him. May it be an inspiration to you and fill your life with love and joy and peace.

Gail Northe

1. *Sri Ramakrishna—the Great Master* by Swami Saradananda, p. 745, pp. 587-88.
2. Bill Moyers—*A World of Ideas*, pp. 241-42.

INTRODUCTION

Form comes into existence from the Infinite like a spark out of fire, in different shapes, structures and molds. All comes forth from That One ever present Spirit; and all ultimately find rest in That. It exists within the very heart and consciousness of each one. It is formless, unbounded, eternal. It is never born nor does It ever die. It always has been and always will be. There is nothing that exists without That. Although He is limitless yet He is the very soul of our souls. We turn east, west, north, south, upward and downward—all is permeated by Him. All that grows on earth, everything that is created, living, moving, unmoving, all have been evolved out of that One.

This is the most wonderful conception of the Deity. It gives a death blow to any limited idea of God or Truth, and whenever we can rise above a restricted viewpoint we have the chance to find unity; we see God manifested not only through ourselves but in all forms. Then no more can we dislike anything, nor shrink from anyone. We become universal by breaking down all the barriers of dogmatism and bigotry.

INTRODUCTION

Among all the difficult problems which perplex the human intellect, the most difficult is man himself. Whence has he come? Whither is he going? Is this the whole of his life or does he continue to live after death? The past is invisible, the future is invisible; he stands helpless in an ever-shifting present, not knowing why he is here or what power is guiding him. He sees all around him differences in character and conditions; some healthy, happy and prosperous; others miserable, perhaps even penniless and starving. Why these inequalities? Is the Lord partial? If some are happy and others unhappy, there must be a reason.

Paramananda[1]

Experience is the only source of knowledge. In the world, religion is the only science where there is no surety, because it is not taught as a science of experience. This should not be. There is always, however, a small group of men who teach religion from experience. They are called mystics, and these mystics in every religion speak the same tongue and teach the same truth. This is the real science of religion.

Vivekananda[1]

Modern Science is the best commentary on the Vedas. The Vedas means right knowledge. The word is derived from Vid, "to know", just as science also comes from the verb meaning "to know". What is the difference between modern science and the whole transcendental science of the Vedas? The method is the same; but modern science moves over the surface only, while the Vedas go deep into the very heart of existence. Modern scientists analyzed and found that the world was made up of atoms, or as they now (1912) declare of electrons. What is an atom or an electron? They do not say. They do not take us beyond that. It is as if it were preached, "Thus far and no farther". They go to a certain distance and beyond that they do not go. Again, according to modern science the world is wholly material. But matter is always darkness; therefore, modern science, so long as it deals with the material realm only, must lead us to darkness, to more and more confusion. Matter leads to matter; but never to spirit; so through matter spirit cannot be known.

It is not possible to know the Infinite through the finite. We must first realize that we ourselves are infinite. For a finite mind it is impossible to conceive of the Supreme Being. You may hold that your mind, although finite, has an infinite potentiality of improvement. But let us see. Granted that it may go on indefinitely knowing facts. You may learn a great number this year; you may know still more next year; in one hundred years you may have learned more, and after a cycle a countless number. But always the number known, however great, must be a finite number, and compared to in-finity will be infinitely small.

Matter is that which is limited and which limits. Man now feels limited by coming in contact with matter. We must know that we are not matter but spirit. We must cease to identify ourselves with this gross material body. We must join ourselves to God. When a man does this and realizes his true Self, then all doubts are dispelled, all questions are answered and he realizes the Highest.

Swami Ramakrishnananda[1]

Anglicized intellectuals—the Hindus I call Englishmen, who whistle European tunes and climb the stairs two at a time, wearing leather riding boots—are always insisting that one should first en-gage in scientific study of the universe and then, on that basis, think about God. But Mother comes first, then the manifestation of Divine Radiance which they call the universe. After attaining God-con-sciousness, all phenomenal structures become trans-parent. Then alone can deep scientific study begin. One can only know the universe by first knowing God, thereby discovering the astonishing fact that it is timeless, spaceless Divine Reality which appears as a universe in space and time. One must meet

Mother Mahamaya, who projects this universal appearance for the education and delight of souls, who
are themselves simply rays of Her Light. By knowing
the Mother Reality first, the mind does not become
obsessed or veiled by partial forms of knowing—
whether through the senses or by various methods of
reasoning. The mind thus becomes free to conduct
true research, which is the unveiling of Oneness—on
every level, in every direction or dimension. By
knowing Divine Oneness, you know the ground of
every possible manifestation, the origin and the harmony of all phenomena. If you inscribe fifty zeros after the numeral one, you are indicating a very large
number, but if you erase the numeral one, nothing
remains. First write the numeral one—first realize
God-consciousness—then inscribe however many zeros you may wish.

Ramakrishna from *Great Swan*[2]

The whole structure of the religious life
is to take man within. When man has exhausted all
that is outside, then he goes within. So Christ said,
"The kingdom of heaven is within." And Sri Krishna
tells us in the Bhagavad-Gita:

> *He whose joy is within, whose bliss*
> *is within, whose light is within,*
> *that devotee, who is all full of*
> *God, attaineth to oneness with God.*

INTRODUCTION

So long as we stay on the outside, we worship Mannon. When we go inside we worship God.

Fear vanishes when we find wisdom and wisdom is inside ourselves. Life in the world is one of constant suffering; but he who knows his Self lives in peace and bliss. Therefore it is said:

> *Ye shall know the Truth and*
> *the Truth shall make you free.*

We do not have to die to attain freedom. We must be free here. And how? By finding the Real within ourselves. The external universe is only the projection, the manifestation, of the internal. The more we learn to know that inner universe of the spirit, the more shall we understand the outer one; and it is this knowledge which will bring us freedom and true happiness. Go within, therefore; find the Real; then live in peace and blessedness.

Paramananda[1]

. . . the time is coming when these thoughts will be cast abroad over the whole world. Instead of living in monasteries, instead of being confined to books of philosophy to be studied only by the learned, instead of being the exclusive possession of sects and of a few of the learned, they will be sown broadcast over the whole world, so that they may become the common property of the saint and the sinner, of men and women and children, of the learned and of the ignorant. They will then permeate the atmosphere of the world, and the very air that we breathe will say with every one of its pulsations, "Thou art That". And the whole universe with its myriads of suns and moons, through everything that speaks, with one voice will say, "Thou art That."

Vivekananda[3]

1. Excerpts from Paramananda, Ramakrishnananda, and Vivekananda—*Message of the East.*
2. Excerpt from *Great Swan—Meetings with Ramakrishna*, Lex Hixon, p. 293.
3. Excerpt from Vivekananda, *The Complete Works of Vivekananda*, Vol. II, p. 288.

THE PROBLEM UNIVERSAL
Lecture by Swami Saradananda
(Delivered in Calcutta)

India is the land whence arose the first anthem of peace and harmony that travelled over the then known world. It was here that the first note of tolerance and of the unity and common brotherhood of all religions was sounded. It was here that arose that joyful song whose keynote was goodwill to all and respect for every opinion which man holds sacred and dear, even today throughout the world; for the hallowed *Rishis* of India had no words of adverse criticism for any individual or system of thought which helped any one to build up his own self, but only soothing notes of peace and toleration and harmony and sympathy. It was in India that the three cardinal principles of religion: *Damyata, Datta, Dayadhvam* (Control and regulate your appetites, Be charitable, Be tolerant and compassionate towards others), were held high as ideals of human life from the Himalayas to Cape Comorin, from the East coast to the West. And it is my belief, in which perhaps you all share, that it is from India again that the first note of universal tolerance will go out over the civilized world, teaching men once more that Universal Brotherhood and Unity which lie beneath all the different forms of religion and philosophy and which the world has forgotten so hopelessly at the present day.

1

From whatever standpoint it is considered, you will find the problem which we have met to discuss is of great importance and vital interest. It arose in the mind of the first-born man in the far beyond where history is dumb and mythology sheds none of her uncertain rays, in these four words: "Whence, How, What and Why?" and we can very rightly put the same question in the same four words today in all the present-day light of reason and science and advancement. The universe stands a constant challenge to the human understanding, and the heart of man has been asking in all times an interpretation of his surroundings, called in one word "Nature." Our science, politics and religion, our sociology, ethics and philosophy, our beliefs about sin and atonement, right and wrong, God-vision and realization of the highest end— all these things which have helped to chasten, purify, ennoble and uplift humanity and are so dear to all our hearts, all these are the outcome of this and this alone. Man finds himself in this vast world surrounded by this infinite environment. He finds himself always acted upon by forces that are lying outside and the action and reaction between these outside forces, the physical or the natural, and those that are to be found within the consciousness of man, is the producer of all knowledge and civilization.

All complexities of thought and action, the result of the accumulations of ages and of varying conditions, have their root in this one problem of all times. Man asked himself repeatedly, What is this universe? Whence is it? How has it come? What is its end? Questions like these came pouring into his mind and perplexed and bewildered, or ennobled and enriched his life in the long run. Ignore them however he might, he could never rid himself of them. Aye, none can give these questions up even at the present day. All men are bound to enquire, explain and act according to the interpretation they put upon them. That has been the law since the beginning of creation and that will be the law in all time to come.

From the interpretation of this one problem—What is the universe?—will come out as necessary conclusions all the different beliefs regarding God, the soul, the life beyond, and everything which we find in the religions, bibles and philosophies of the world. If we could examine the history of the different interpretations given in different ages through the crude and simple language of mythology, or through the well-balanced, precise, yet expressive language of philosophy and science, it would be a very interesting study. But for our present purpose I shall try to put before you the solution of the great Indian sages of old and compare it with the conclusions which the modern world of thought have come to, and see how far the old conclusions agree with the new ones.

All the answers given as explanations of the objective world can be divided into two principal classes. One holds that atoms are the ultimate cause of this universe; molecules are formed by a force called molecular attraction inherent in the atoms, and out of their aggregate has come all these wonderful varied objects which we see before us. Now if we are able to admit this theory, then the atoms of the materialists must have possessed in the germ state, amongst others, the qualities of consciousness and intelligence which, gradually developed and highly refined, appeared at last as human consciousness and intelligence; and not only that, but they must have had the power of organization and the will to evolve into all these things. To scientists who believe that such intelligent matter is the ultimate cause of this universe we have nothing to say. For they speak in different words only of the same principles which men have been calling God or an ever-guiding Intelligence; and therefore this atomic theory virtually coincides with the theory that God is the cause of this universe.

There is another group of thinkers holding a different opinion,—that everything is the outcome of mental vibration. All that I know, all these objects around me are nothing but my own mental images. The sensations and perceptions are all in my own mind and I conclude wrongly that the outside objects and the world are producing them in me. This has been called Idealism. Now here, too, we find on examination that, to show that the mind is the cause of this universe, we shall have to prove that the mind is independent of outside impressions and that it can create all and any of the images at will. But is this true? Can we bring out any new combination, anything that we desire, out of our own minds? Certanly not. And so we find that this theory also must have a defect in some part or other. Then there is another thing. Can or do we ever know matter as separate from or independent of the mind and mental forces? Certainly not. No scientist has been able to analyse and separate matter and force. The combination of the two is there even in the smallest particle which he calls atom; and the scientist's mind has been there to give an interpretation. On the other hand, there are many who agree in thinking that atoms are nothing but so many centres of force. The actions of what we call force or energy are what give them their appearance and individuality as atoms.

Hindu philosophy considers mind as a subtle material force, but not the spirit. The mind works through the medium of the brain, and is in its own turn an instrument in the hand of the soul. The process of life and thought does not die with the death of the body, but it passes on with the soul; and when the soul takes another body, it goes on working and gathering experience again through the medium of that body. A beautiful expression of this principle comes in the fifteenth chapter of the Bhagavad-Gita:—"Whatever body is entered into, or whatever body is departed from, the Lord takes them (the mind and the senses, etc.,) along with him like the wind (carrying) the scents off from their seats (flowers, etc.)". And the conclusion of the Hindu philosophy has always been that the mind can be enlarged, developed and expanded to an infinite extent. We can see the soul only through itself in the state of superconscious existence; once there, all fetters drop off, all limitations vanish forever; the activities of the finite and the limited stop and the infinite shines out in its everlasting power and glory.

We find both these theories of materialism and idealism—the attempts to explain the origin of the universe from matter or from mind alone, however good they may be in other respects, are inconclusive and unsatisfactory to human reason; hence they are both defective. Aye, the Hindu Seers differ considerably in their opinion about this. What is their conclusion then, about the subject and the object, mind and matter, the knower and the known? They say that all these are manifestations of one Eternal Unit,—the witness that is behind. They have come out of One Substance, which is the *Akhanda Satchidananda*—the indivisible and hence unlimited essence of Existence, Knowledge and Bliss. Mistake them not when they say that it is *the* indivisible principle of Existence, Knowledge and Bliss. Knowledge and existence and love, as we know them, are all finite. And why have they been qualified by the old *Rishis* with the words indivisible, infinite or unbounded? Because human language is too imperfect to express that Eternal Witness that is behind the inner and outer manifestations. Speech and mind can never reach There, because they are the effects of It. "Whence speech falls back baffled, with the mind"—such is the nature of the Unit behind and thus has it been extolled by the voice of the Vedas and Upanishads. The One Eternal Substance is always behind, and That has brought to light the subject and the object. Hence it can never be known by the mind. Herbert Spencer's "Unknowable" thus approaches very near to the "Substance" of the Hindu *Rishis*. The great difference, however, lies in this: that the Hindu *Rishis* hold that it is quite possible for man to attain to It and realize fully his oneness with It; and the attainment of that stage has been called by them the stage of *Nirvikalpa Samadhi,*—the state of Super-conscious Existence. In this there are no more wanderings of the mind after things that wither and perish, but it remains calm and satisfied in the realization of the nature and glory of the Soul. The old Seers of the Vedas never treated the different stages of consciousness as separate things. They came to know by introspection, of which the different methods are to be found in the different philosophical systems, that the three stages of consciousness supplement, but never contradict one another. The subconscious existence that we find in the lower animals and in still lower organisms, the consciousness as it exists in man and in beings higher than man, and then the highest stage of consciousness, the superconscious existence—all these have never been looked upon as the functions of three different minds, but as different conditions or stages of One Mind. Self-consciousness is a step in advance of the subconscious stage towards development and progress, and reaches its perfection in the superconscious existence. Indeed there is no difference between them except in degree.

We have seen that the universe can never be the result of atoms or material particles. We have seen also that the universe cannot be the outcome of mind alone. The Hindu Sages beautifully express this view in a sublime verse in the Katha-Upanishad;—"The universe is like an everlasting fig tree having its roots high up in the bosom of the Infinite and its branches here below." To find the root of this universe you will have to go beyond time, space and causation; because the roots are fixed there in the bosom of the Infinite. Then the verse goes on to say: "That is Pure, that is Brahman, that is Immortal." Therefore the first thing that we find regarding the universe is that it has been projected out of that Absolute Existence which forms the background of it. Then again there is another thing. They have looked upon this universe as one homogeneous whole. Outside we have this ocean of matter connecting everything that is material. Our bodies are like so many whirlpools in the ocean of matter and are always linked with the sun and the moon and other beings (if there are any) in the other planets. Behind this ocean of matter what do we find? The ocean of mind. Your mind and my mind and the mind of everyone here or elsewhere exist in that mental ocean and are thus joined together. They are like so many centres of force in the one vast ocean of mind, and beyond that there lies the Infinite, the Absolute—that which can never be described by any word, nor be reached by the limited mind. It transcends all limits, but the reflection of that One Soul falls upon all these different centres of force in the mental ocean. We have seen how millions of reflections, produced by one sun in the millions of waves in the ocean, appear as so many different suns. Even where the water is muddy, there is the reflection, only we do not see it. And so the reflection of that One Soul is shining within you and me and within everyone. The reflection within you forms your individuality, your little ego, and so on with all the rest. But in reality there is but One Soul pervading everything; and if we can transcend the limits of the mind and the body, we shall reach the Real Truth. But the Vedanta philosophy never says that all these reflections are false. The *Rishis* did not say that the reflections do not exist or that the relative world, because it is a phenomenon, is an illusion. It exists, but relatively. As long as there will be relativity, there will be this world; but outside of this relativity there will be found One Infinite Ocean of Knowledge and Love reigning supreme, there will be found the One without a second. The knower and the known, the subject and the object and all these varied differentiations come under the same category of relativity and have been projected out of One Principle of Existence. This, therefore, is the interpretation of the universe: that it is the outcome of something which is not relative but absolute in its essence. The scientists of the present age have also come to the same conclusion: that all these phenomena can never exist unless they are based on some permanent principle—a groundwork upon which all colors have been drawn. Materialism says there is nothing but matter. Idealism says there is nothing but mind. But the Vedanta says: No, mind and matter are manifestations of one Permanent Substance; they are the outcome of One Permanent Essence which can be best described as the Infinite Ocean of Knowledge and Bliss. "Verily, out of Bliss has this universe evolved, it lives in Bliss and in Bliss does it go back and is absorbed. Know *Brahman* to be Bliss."

This is the conclusion of the Vedas. It follows from this that the knowledge and happiness that we find within ourselves are the conditioned manifestations of the Infinite Knowledge and Bliss. But because they are coming to us through the conditions of time, space and causation, we can see but little of that Infinite Knowledge and get only a partial and often distorted view of it.

Now let us come to the second question: How has it come out? Evolution forms the backbone of the Hindu Religion. Evolution is there through and through in the doctrines of the Vedas. The great philosopher and the father of Indian Psychology, Kapila, discovered it, and in his system, which is called the *Sankhya* philosophy, we find the origin and the process of the growth of the universe explained through evolution. The process of cosmic evolution as

known and taught by the scientists of the day, agrees
in main with that of the *Sankhya* system, though of
course there is a want of detail in the latter. But there is
a great difference between the scientists of the present
day and the philosophers of India. The latter hold that
if evolution is true, involution must also be equally
true; and does not science tend to prove it through her
own methods? No force can proceed in a direct line, but
comes round and completes the circle, if it does not
meet with any resistance on the way and is given sufficient time for it. All force comes round to the place
from which it started; and is not that a proof of the
fact that if evolution is true, involution must be true,
too? If the world has come out of a Permanent Substance, it is sure to go back into It in the long run. This
wave of evolution and involution is going on from all
eternity, and there is no beginning of this process. How
is it possible, you may ask, that there should be no
beginning of creation? The question itself involves a big
fallacy, for it implies that you want to know the beginning of the cause which has produced this universe, for
if the cause is there from all eternity, the effect must
have been synchronous with it; and if the effect has a
real beginning, the cause has a beginning too. We all
know that this universe is relative. We see all these
motions and changes in everything here; indeed, constant change or motion is the law of it. Is not time itself
a relative thing? What is time but a relative idea that
comes to us through the changes that are going on in
our minds; so the idea of space, too, comes in that way
relatively. No one can say that the ideas of time and
space are absolute, however much they may be ingrained
in us. Everyone knows and all philosophers agree that

the little child has no idea of distance at all. If we place a red thing before it, it will first put its hand in its own eyes, and then farther and farther away as the idea of distance unfolds through experience from its struggles to get at the thing. Therefore, to find an answer to this question—at what time precisely creation began—we shall have to go beyond time and know that which is beyond time, hence absolute, and that is not possible for human reason.

What is God then? We have seen how the Hindu Sages emphatically declare that the Absolute Essence of Existence can be realized by man when he transcends the limits of time, space and causation. But so long as he is under these limitations, he cannot have a full view of It; he gets only a fragmentary glimpse; and this par-tial vision of the Absolute is what is to be understood by God. Let us illustrate this by an example. We see the sun above. Science tells us that the sun is many million times larger than the earth we inhabit, and yet we see the sun there as a bright little disc. Do we see the real sun or not? The answer will be that we do and do not. How is that possible? We see the real sun, but not as it really is, in shape, size and nature. Now let us imagine that we are travelling by a railway train or a balloon towards the luminary. With every step in advance, our vision of the sun is changed; we see it larger and brighter. The light and the heat go on increasing as we come nearer to it; then finally when we reach our desti-nation, we see the sun as it is. Therefore, what we saw from the earth was both true and untrue. It was the vision of the real sun, and it was not; that is, it was not the full view of the sun, but a partial one. So is the case with the idea of God. In whatever physical and mental plane man may be placed, he can never lose sight entirely of the vision of the Self, the Witness within, in Whom he is living and moving and having his being. Just as we are seeing the one real sun all the time, so we are feeling the existence of that Eternal, Unchangeable Ocean of Knowledge and Bliss within us, however much the vision may be dimmed or distorted by our surrounding conditions. Wherever we may have been placed through the process of evolution, we have been trying to approach it all the time.

As we evolve higher and higher, our ideas of God go on developing and becoming greater and greater; and it is in this way that all the various ideas of God have come into existence in this world. Believe me, all these ideas of God are not false, neither are they all suited to one particular mind at the same time; but they will be found to suit different minds in their different stages of growth and development. Vedanta teaches that the idea of a God immanent in nature and creation is but a partial manifestation of Him. This is *Iswara*, whose body is this wonderful universe, and whose mind is the sum total of all minds. Do we not find the same idea in the world of thought today in the West? Can that idea be possibly grasped by a Stone Age man? Certainly not. He has his own ideas and becomes a fetichist or an animist or polytheist according to his own development. He worships his ancestors, and through the constant push of the ever-flowing current of evolution, his religious instinct expands, and he comes to recognize other gods presiding over the various functions of nature. Finally, as his mind develops and his perception grows keener, he comes to the ideas of monotheism and monism. Why does the Vedantist have not a single word of reproach or abuse for any idea of God, however crude it might be, though he himself worships the One *Iswara* immanent in nature? Because he is the greatest believer in God and knows that it will never do to force any one idea of the Deity on all, irrespective of individual development; and so he wants to keep intact all the different ideas of God grown through different ages and suited to different states of the human mind. He will never say that the highest idea of God will never be reached by even the lowest man on earth. Everyone is sure to come to it in time. Let him worship, therefore, according to his present beliefs. Let him have his idea and do you hold to your own. Let us all bear in mind that there is an ever-guiding hand in this universe, a beneficent power which is leading each one of us higher and higher; so that, in the long run, no one will be kept back from the highest stage of development. All the higher ideas of God which have come to any one of us will be the property of all. They will all evolve from out their own real Self, which is the Deity Itself.

The principal point which the Vedantist urges is that all knowledge is within us. It can never be outside of us. But there are barriers which prevent its coming out; and what does education mean but the removal of these barriers? How could you make a child grasp an idea? Only by removing the obstructions that are in its way and the idea will come out and manifest itself. This has been the basis of the modern educational system. Examine the kindergarten method and the different systems which have been discovered lately, and you will find that this is the case. They are not trying to hammer into the child's brain any idea, but they are all the time teaching it the use of its own powers and the knowledge is coming out of itself. You can do nothing else but this. Therefore, it is very true that all knowledge and power are within and not without us. The only thing required is to build up our will to bring them out. They may be brought out by different means, but constant longing alone must be the condition of all these means. They can come out by controlling the mind and by the conservation of energy, which is the one principle common to all the systems of Yoga. We all know the law of hydrostatics; that if there are eight holes in a bladder and the bladder is full of water, and if you stop seven of them, the water will come out through the remaining one with the combined force of eight. Yoga in a few words is nothing else but the stoppage of the flow of the mental energy through more than one desired channel. Earnest and heartfelt prayers, too, will bring the powers of the soul out. For what can be stronger than the prayers of a devoted mind?

Another point which the Vedantist wishes to urge on us is this—that man struggles not from error to truth, but that he has been proceeding all the time from lower to higher truths, and all these are like so many steps of the ladder of evolution by which he is rising up to the highest. The lower truths, like the lower steps, may not be necessary for one who has risen a good way, but they are unavoidably necessary for those who are still down below. Thus flows the course of evolution, and man rises by catching hold of truth after truth and ideal after ideal, till at last he reaches the end. We have no idea of absolute truth at present. Truth, as it appears to us, is relative; hence we find its gradations from lower to higher and from higher to the highest; and blessed is he who recognizes this fact. His toleration and sympathy and active help to others know no bounds. India alone of all places recognized this truth from prehistoric times, and it is also an historical fact that there has not been a single religious persecution in this land of toleration. It is here that monism attained its highest stage; and from this land this sublime truth has been and still will be spread all round.

"He is the All and the Over-all. He is the relative and yet He far transcends the relative." The whole universe forms the body of God, the infinite mind is His mind, and in His absolute nature He is the essence of the soul of all beings. He is the God immanent in nature, working in and through all these physical and mental forces, and yet He transcends all. This is, in brief, the idea of God as conceived by the Vedantist. Now comes the idea of man. If man is a part of the Highest Self, that Absolute Being that forms the basis of this universe, what difference is there between God and man? The difference is this: God is almighty, the sum total of all minds forms His mind; whereas man has but a limited mind which forms, as it were, one single eddy in the infinite ocean of mind, and hence he knows but little, and his power is limited. But when he will recognize his real nature, he will be one with the Infinite Deity. The essence of all beings and the essence of God are one and the same. The difference is in the degree of manifestation. The Creator transcends all the limits of time, space and causation, which bind the little mind of man. But man will attain to that absolute state as soon as he will feel himself one with Him. This has been proved again and again in the lives of all the great teachers of the different religions. A beautiful illustration of man's thus gaining the God-consciousness comes in one of the Upanishads, of which I shall give you a free rendering. Two birds having a beautiful plumage are sitting on this tree of life—the one above sitting majestic in its own glory and not caring to taste the sweet and bitter fruits thereof. As the lower one gets the bitter taste of certain fruits, it becomes disgusted and looks up at the bright vision above and proceeds towards it, overpowered by its glorious light. But the alluring fruits entice it again before it has proceeded far on its journey, and it goes on tasting the fruits as before. Again it gets the taste of a bitter fruit, and in its disgust looks up and is charmed by the sweet vision above. Again it gives up and proceeds on its way. Disgusted and charmed, forgetting and remembering, it thus draws nearer and nearer to the upper bird; when it is close enough, lo! the whole vision changes and it finds itself one with the upper bird. It sees itself glorious and effulgent and the lower bird appears to be but its own shadow. Thus in the two verses of the Upanishad is shown the process of development of the finite individuality of man into the Infinite Self of God—the Oneness, as it has been termed, with God.

The question arises: Is it not Pantheism, what we have been preaching? What if it is Pantheism, if by it I feel the existence of God nearer than by the so-called Theism or any other Ism? There are different stages of Pantheism. There is one stage of Pantheism which is nothing else but materialism. It teaches that God has changed into this material universe, and everything that we find here is a part of God, and there is no other God except this manifested universe. This is not the Pantheism of the Vedanta. The Vedanta wants man to become identified with the Infinite Love of God and to make him forget his little self entirely. Is this Pantheism? The materialistic Pantheism is not at all a suitable name for the religion of the Vedanta; you might express it better by the word Hypertheism or Supertheism, or something higher than Theism. The God of the so-called Theism is outside this world. Vedanta leads us a step higher and proclaims the immanency of God in and through all this creation and process of evolution, and so we might better term it Hypertheism, Supertheism or Monism. Let us not cast truth away because it has been labelled with the bad name of Pantheism; but let us be humble votaries at the shrine of Truth, wherever it may be found, be it in the Vedas, or in the Bible of the Christians, or in the brilliant researches of Modern Science.

Of the four questions, we have considered the answer of two,—"Whence?" and "How?" The other two remain—"What?" and "Why?" What is this universe for? And the answer comes clear: To take each and every one to the highest point of evolution—that is the end of the universe. To evolve life and consciousness even in the lowest particle and take it to the highest, the superconscious existence, where man will find no more barriers to his knowledge—barriers which his material body and mind are constantly manufacturing—that is the end of the universe. But why has the Creator projected this universe out of Himself? Necessity He has none, or if He has any, would it not mean a certain imperfection in Him? Nobody can answer this "Why." But this question, too, involves a fallacy. Man has been asking this "Why" from time immemorial. In old times, when his power of thought was immature, he had to satisfy himself by bringing out those crude theories of creation which are to be found in the mythologies of the world. Later on, when his power grew, he put the same question thus: How has the conditioned come from the unconditioned; or how has the unlimited become the limited? We have been forgetting over and over again that in order to find the answer to this we shall have to go beyond and transcend all relativity; because you will find it in the Absolute and nowhere else. Vedanta explains this question from two positions. The one is the standpoint of relativity and the other that of the Absolute entity or the standpoint of God Himself. From the standpoint of relativity there might be a necessity of Theology; but from the standpoint of God, the answer is that there is no universe in our sense of the word. And why? Because God finds Himself to be all these things and knows that. He is yourself, myself and everybody else's self, but knows them not as separate entities. He knows that He it is Himself alone who is manifesting and playing, and there is none else separate from Him, and therefore He cannot be said to be conscious of creation as a separate thing from Himself. Thus arises the doctrine of the *Vivartavada* of the Vedanta, which later on, misunderstood and misinterpreted, gave birth to the crude illusory theory of the universe, as we find it in the translations of our Scriptures by Western scholars. The truth is, the Vedanta tries to give no explanation from the Absolute standpoint except that the world is a spontaneous outflow of the Deity, a play of love of the Infinite with Himself.

From the relative point of view there is every necessity of creation as we have seen before, and this

relativity will remain true so long as there is this relative vision. The necessity of creation from the human
standpoint is to lead man higher and higher till at
length he brings out all the powers that are hidden
within him, which all of us are going to do some day
or other. Let me now conclude with a prayer from the
Vedas: "May our mind and speech act in harmony
with that Highest Truth. Do Thou, Oh Self-effulgent
Light, reveal Thyself to us! May the senses bring and
retain day and night the higher light which has
been revealed through the Scriptures. I shall speak what
I know to be true, and may that truth protect and
perfect him who speaks as well as him who hears. Peace,
Peace, Peace!"

*There is no philosophy in the world that is
not indebted to Kapila. Pythagoras came to India and
studied this philosophy, and that was the beginning of the
philosophy of the Greeks. Later, it formed the Alexandrian
school, and still later, the Gnostic. It became divided into
two; one part went to Europe and Alexandria, and the
other remained in India; and out of this, the system of
Vyasa was developed. The Sankhya philosophy of Kapila
was the first rational system that the world ever saw. Every
metaphysician in the world must pay homage to him...
This wonderful man, the most ancient of philosophers is
mentioned even in the Shruti: "O Lord, Thou who produced
the sage Kapila in the beginning."*

Vivekananda

THE INDIAN MIND AND INDIAN CULTURE
by Sister Devamata

he profoundly subjective development of the Indian mind is not based, as many suppose, on an innate tendency to visionary dreaming, but on acute practical observation of nature. Their science of the invisible is as exact and empirical as Western science of the natural. Their impetus towards the inner, in fact, sprang from their study of the outer. As far as they could reach on the outside, so far they travelled, observing at every step that macrocosm and microcosm ran in parallel lines. When they could move no further outward, they turned inward, trusting that the same correspondence would obtain. As before, they had learned the law from the macrocosm and found its application in the microcosm; now, forced back by the illusive character of nature on the study of their own inner being, they began to dissect and analyze the microcosm and from that central point penetrate still deeper into the hidden mysteries of the macrocosm. Everywhere the analogy between the two seemed to hold. Thus it was that the first understanding of themselves came through observation of nature; while a deeper study of their own organism enabled them to discover secrets of the natural world forever hidden from the scientist who depends upon microscope or dissecting knife.

21

Recognizing that they already held within their grasp an instrument more efficient than any man could invent, they set out to unfold all the inherent possibilities of the human mind, and developed a power of concentration and subjective observation such probably as has never been surpassed in this world. They surprised nature at work. They saw the great machine of the universe in motion, and were able to discover and study the relative position and function of each part. It was from the living man, the living animal that they learned their lessons; but not as modern science has accomplished it through the horrors of vivisection. That was contrary to the whole spirit of their civilization. It seemed to them a poor achievement merely to draw a map of the human organism; to discover the plan of the nervous system, the place of vein and muscle and tendon. They must see the nerve currents flash their message along the fine wires of grey matter; they must follow the swift-flowing stream of blood through its ramified course; they must watch from breath to breath the effect on mind and body of the great pumping system of the lungs. It was a living, pulsing world which interested them, not a dead mechanism; and the only instrument which could unveil it was a living instrument. The intelligence, they argued, which has evolved through such countless stages from the lowest forms of life, must have the power to review its own work. Hence for the fully developed and focused mind there could be nothing hidden. Like a searchlight, or an X-ray, it should pierce the densest veil of matter. It should be able to penetrate into the heart of all things, above all into the nature and constitution of man himself. The perfect scientist therefore must be a Seer.

As a result, preparation for scientific investigation among them was less in the laboratory than out in the forest or in some solitary mountain fastness. As M. Brieux, a member of the French Academy, writes: "The noble minds of India, without having had the necessity of having recourse to experimental science like us, discovered the truths which we discover after them. By the unaided power of meditation, they have given an explanation of the universe which appeared ridiculous to us for a long time, but which our scholars are now beginning to accept." Thus Kapila, who lived in the 7th or 8th century B.C. and who is regarded as the father of all systematic philosophic and scientific thought in India, was a *Sadhu*, a man of renunciation and profound spiritual understanding. It was not merely by empirical research, but through long hours of deep meditation that he uncovered the secrets of the physical as well as of the metaphysical universe— facts which one by one are being verified by modern science. With a power of penetration derived from a perfectly concentrated mental vision, he perceived that the atomic theory could not be the last word of the physicist, that there were finer units of matter which he named "force-centres." And today we talk of electrons! Without caustic pencil and burning candle, he discovered that matter cannot be annihilated; that destruction is nothing but "reversion to the causal state"; that "the effect is only the cause reproduced"; that "something cannot come out of nothing"; "that the laws of nature are regular and uniform through-out." More than all, he anticipated Herbert Spencer in enunciating and developing the theory of evolution with such definiteness as to draw from Huxley the admission: "To say nothing of Hindu Sages to whom evolution was a familiar notion, ages before Paul of Tarsus was born."

Nor were he and his followers content, like Western evolutionists, to leave their theory at loose ends, carried only to the far boundary of the gross physical realm, with the whole of man's higher nature unaccounted for. It is the characteristic of the Hindu mind to push every theory to its ultimate conclusion, not to stop short of the furthest confines of individual consciousness. Having followed the germ of life through its slow upward course from the protoplasmic cell to the human body, those great Aryan Seers found that only the first stage of its journey was completed; that, as Tyndall admitted at the close of his life, there lay beyond a vast unexplored region, where the laws of the lower realm,—struggle for existence, survival of the fittest—were reversed. Through that, too, the scientist must travel with the evolving germ, they said, if he would make his investigations complete. So they moved onward, and as they watched the unfoldment of the intellectual and then the spiritual consciousness and realized that, if it had taken eons to evolve a human body, how insufficient must one span of life be to evolve a soul, they gradually formulated the doctrines of *Karma* and Reincarnation, without which, Schopenhauer states, there can be no logical explanation of the universe. The first is merely the law of cause and effect applied not only to man's physical body, but to that subtler body of character which clothes the moral man; and the other is but the process of evolution extended to the whole of his nature and life.

Thus it was that in the Vedanta, religion and science rose from the same base,—the law of causation and evolution. And ever since they have stood firmly together as two inherent parts of one structure, never a house divided against itself. Conflict between religion and science is an unknown thing in India. As a great Hindu spiritual teacher once said to me: "The struggle for Truth on the outside is what we call science; the struggle for Truth on the inside is what we call religion." But since Truth is one, there can be no variance between them. Science is the foundation; religion is the superstructure; and philosophy is that which binds the two together, which correlates the facts of both and unites them into a complete whole.

It is this quality of completeness, of inclusiveness, which characterizes all Indo-Aryan thought. Nothing is left hanging in mid-air, nothing is taken for granted, nothing is omitted. The Hindu truthseeker in his researches realized that every fact in the universe must be accounted for. To leave out one was to render all science hypothetical. Yet to try to compass the whole realm of external phenomena was, he knew, an impossibility. Hence the only method was to pierce through phenomena to the Noumenon, to find that "knowing which all else would be known"; to leave untrammelled the diversity of nature and to penetrate to the unity behind. It was the determined effort of those ancient Vedic *Rishis* to find the point of unity in the midst of this infinite variety which led to their extreme subjectivity. They understood that all investigation must be concentric, that only in the

Final Cause could all things meet; and seeking that, they mounted step by step the ladder of Abstract Truth until they attained heights of idealism such that Max Muller declares: "None of our philosophers, not excepting Heraclitus, Plato, Kant or Hegel, has ventured to erect such a spire, never frightened by storms or lightnings. Stone follows on stone, in regular succession after once the first step has been made, after once it has been clearly seen that in the beginning there can have been but One, as there will be but One in the end, whether we call it *Atman* or *Brahman*."

Yet they were not mere idealists, as it is too often claimed. Standing at a great distance, we see only the tallest pinnacle of any structure. So with the Vedic teaching. Looking back through the long vista of the ages, the ordinary observer perceives the high-est points of Indian philosophy only and characterizes it as pure speculative idealism. But those who draw closer, discover beneath those lofty towers of idealistic thought a solid edifice of science and reason. The facts of history bear this out. It is known today that all the sciences made great strides in ancient India and some of them point to it as their birthplace. The Greeks borrowed much of their *Materia Medica* from the Hindus. Chemistry with them was a well-developed science and it was from them, so Dr. Royle declares, that the Arabs learned the use of metals as internal remedies. The code of Manu stands as a model to the world of law, and Sanskrit grammar is acknowledged to be the most perfect grammar known. In mathematics the Hindus discovered geometry and the use of algebra in astronomical investigations and geometrical demon-strations. It was they who gave to the Arabs the Decimal Notation, which made Arithmetic for both East and West a practical science; and later on, their great astronomer, Ary-Bhatta (476 A.D.), who is called the Newton of India, proclaimed the law of gravitation and calculated the distance of the earth's circumference.

The ruins of astronomical observatories, the records of ancient laboratory and library, show that the Indo-Aryans did not disregard the value of the empirical method. On the contrary, no modern scientist has held to it with such rigid insistence; for they claimed that it was not enough to apply it merely to the realm of outer nature, it must be carried with equal precision into the realm of religion. Experience should be the criterion of higher forms of knowledge as well as lower. Every individual, in fact, should evolve his own religion by experiment and observation. In doing this he could take as his guide any great teacher or Saviour, or he could go boldly on alone, testing the truth of their discoveries and revelations by his own. He must "prove all things" for himself, until the last theory has been merged into a demonstrated fact. Man must not be content to speculate concerning the existence of God, he must see and know Him. Mere belief in immortality will not do: while still in the body each one must find that in him which is deathless and identify himself with that, if he would become immortal. Every phenomenon of his inner being must be tried out in the crucible of experience, else for him there can be no true religion and no living God.

To make this possible was the great achievement of Patanjali, the successor of Kapila. He sought to develop in the field of psychology a scientific system of education by which man could gain full possession of that vast subjective realm beyond the reach of the senses. He saw that so long as the process of evolution was confirmed to the subconscious region, nature could work unhindered and carry the individual germ of life on its way, in passive submission—like a child in its mother's arms. When, however, it rose to the realm of the conscious and became cognizant of itself, a self-conscious being, from that moment it must cooperate with nature, if it would hasten on its way to perfection. How this cooperation might best be accomplished was his chief study and out of it rose the science of Yoga. The word itself is the precursor of the English derivative from the Sanskrit "yoke" and signifies "joining" or "union"; and it was thus applied because the purpose of the science was to effect a union between man's lower and higher being. As nature, unaided, had borne the evolving soul from the subconscious or brute state to the conscious or human; so man must now learn to bridge for himself the chasm lying between the human and the Divine or superconscious. This, he perceived, could be done, not by going against nature, but by working with her,—taking the same processes used by her on the lower plane and employing them on the higher level.

In the West religion has been too often represented as a conflict with nature, a "striving with the Lord." Not so in India. The science of Yoga or religious practice is a natural science; not because it leaves out of account the supernatural, but because in the Vedanta the horizon of the natural is stretched to such ultra-fine limits that beyond stands the Absolute alone. And since religion is the struggle of man to "rebind" himself to God, it necessarily lies within the realm of his finite perception. Therefore religious or superconscious development should be but the continuation of one unbroken system of education beginning with the body and culminating in the soul. Such was the system of Yoga. Through its different branches,—*Hatha, Karma, Raja, Jnana* and *Bhakti*—man was shown how he could unfold the latent powers of body, mind, intellect and heart and come into possession of his whole being. Nor are its methods any more occult or mysterious than are the principles of higher mathematics or the multiform manifestations of electricity. The play of nature's subtler forces must always seem mysterious to the unknowing mind. What will the simple villager think, who without acquaintance with the telephone suddenly hears the voice of a son one hundred miles away? Or who perchance catches out of the air the strains of orchestral music, as did the wireless operator in a coast station when he broke in on the current of a tel-electric organ? All things function according to some law and the true scientist is he who takes account of every plane of nature, not of the sense world only.

So long as science adheres obstinately to the gross material realm, it must be content to see "through a glass darkly". At any moment a new set of phenomena may arise and overturn any one of its theories, as we so often witness. There is but one way for it to see "face to face", that is to stop dealing with effects and begin the study of causes. To do this the scientist must rise to the plane of perception where causal forces operate. There is in the microcosm a plane corresponding to each plane of the macrocosm. Every individual stands, as it were, like a longitudinal section of the whole; and as he rises from stratum to stratum of his own consciousness, he comes into spontaneous understanding of the laws of that stratum in the universe outside. The great Hindu Seers discovered this fact, and it was that which led them to their highly metaphysical development. Yet they did not at any time underrate the value or necessity of all the lower stages through which they had travelled. Max Muller in his *Three Lectures on the Vedanta Philosophy* says: "Nor was there in India any necessity for honest thinkers to screen their doctrines behind the name of Esoteric Religion . . . And what is even more creditable to the ancient believers and philosophers of India, they never, in the exalted position which was allowed to them on account of their superior knowledge and sanctity, looked down with disdain on those who had not yet risen to their own height. They recognized the previous stages of submissive studentship and active citizenship as essential steps towards the freedom which they themselves enjoyed; nay, they admitted no one to their companionship who had not passed through these stages of passive obedience and practical usefulness,"—that is, who had not served his apprenticeship in the life of objective activity.

Everywhere in creation the physical and the metaphysical exist side by side; and the character of a civilization is determined by the preponderance of one or the other, although only in the balanced union of the two does it reach a great height. Indian development has always been preeminently metaphysical. In their unfaltering search for the Essence, the Soul of all things, the Hindus have sharpened both their outer and their inner faculties. Even their senses have become keener, so that, as their minds can discern subtle differences imperceptible to the blunter mind of the West, so their eyes perceive subtler beauties in nature; and it is said that there are nowhere in the world greater nature-lovers than the Hindus. Their ears too can detect finer intervals of sound, which has resulted in so elaborate a system of music that few in the West can grasp it. It was no doubt to satisfy their delicate power of hearing that they invented the violin; and so sensitive are they to harmony in all things that they have different kinds of music for different hours of the day and different seasons of the year, and a song sung out of its hour or season jars upon them like a harsh discord.

In the West, on the other hand, the physical has always predominated. The metaphysical has been relegated to the region of pure speculation. Idealism has been an exotic growth, whose roots have never struck deep into society. Yet this does not mean that the civilization of either East or West is inferior. Both physical and metaphysical are necessary to a complete development. Through the cultivation of his subjective powers only and the consequent attainment of a concentrated inner vision, man can move from effects to causes and learn to apprehend the higher truths of nature; yet without test tube and microscope he cannot hope to demonstrate and teach those truths to others who have not developed like power. Truth is revealed in the world of the metaphysical; it is made practical and universal in the world of the physical. Man perceives Truth by cultivating his metaphysical or spiritual sight; he shares it with his fellowmen by developing his physical resources. The subjective is always individual, the objective alone can become social. But the letter without the spirit killeth; so a well-constructed social and political organism without a true religious consciousness is a body without a soul. The stirring of religious interest throughout the West today shows that it is beginning to recognize this fact. And now as always will it be the province of the East, while learning lessons of material progress from the West, to point out to the occidental world the way to a renewal of subjective or spiritual life.

EVOLUTION AND REVOLUTION
Lecture by Swami Ramakrishnananda

efore I explain what evolution is, it is desirable to give some idea of materialistic monism. Materialists all over the world regard the universe as come out of one substance, and that substance goes by the name of matter. What is Matter? Until recent times it was thought that matter was made up of atoms. But that theory has now been destroyed. Atoms are no longer the smallest particles which make up matter. Electrons are at present the smallest particles. These electrons, being some of them positive and some negative, attract and repel one another and out of this attraction and repulsion, revolution takes place. These revolutions are of different velocity and on account of the various revolutions, atoms of different kinds come into existence. Electrons are all one, but scientists do not think that they are the smallest particles into which matter can be divided. They believe that there are finer particles which are known as ether. However, as far as we have gone, electrons are the smallest particles and it is through their various revolutions that we get our seventy or eighty atoms. Out of atoms molecules come into existence; out of molecules come sensible objects; and out of sensible objects, the whole universe, such as we see it.

Charles Darwin, the greatest naturalist of this age,

believed that out of these atoms life itself was evolved and he finds its first embryonic form in a sort of viscous or granular body which goes by the name of amoeba. This amoeba has some sort of consciousness. Its body is made up of a substance called matter. It has a will to live, so it strives to protect itself. In its efforts to pre-serve life, it develops new and higher characteristics until another species is brought into existence. Through the struggle of this new species for existence, a still stronger species is developed; and so by this process, out of the amoeba comes a fish. But the larger fish wants to swallow the little fish and the little fish tries to run away; it develops a will and in its effort to pre-serve life, the fish becomes a bird. Thus Darwin has pointed out how in this struggle for existence, higher and higher grades of life arise; until the anthropoid ape comes and, at last, man. It is in this manner that he accounts for the existence of a Goethe, a Newton, a Shakespeare. These materialistic scientists do not accept anything that they cannot see or perceive with the senses. According to them, two courses of matter are flowing on,—one conscious, the other unconscious. The stream is always running on and the highest devel-opment of this motion is the human being. Man in turn goes on developing until the highest man arises; but what the highest type of man will be they are not certain.

This, however, is a general evolution. The individual evolution Darwin, Herbert Spencer and their co-work-ers have entirely overlooked. Whether a man continues to exist after death they have never tried to decide. As I said before, all these materialistic philosophers be-lieve that everything has come out of matter. From solid matter has come liquid; from liquid, gases; from gases, ether; and out of luminous ether has come consciousness. This consciousness is evolving and out of it will come a Newton or a Goethe. But when Newton or Goethe dies, what will become of him? The answer is given: They are extinguished. Newton and Goethe no longer exist, but their influence continues to live. They have contributed their quota to universal evolution. This theory, however, is very unsatisfactory, for everyone wills to be. And according to Darwin, out of that will to be has come the struggle for existence; while out of the struggle for existence, the highest forms of life have sprung.

Now, we ask, since this is unsatisfactory, what will finally triumph? Will it be consciousness, or unconsciousness? But if consciousness is the highest development of matter, then it must triumph. What is consciousness? Consciousness means knowledge. For example, Darwin was thinking of his theory of evolution. He kept on thinking and thinking and thus he evolved his theory. But without Charles Darwin, could the theory have come? No. It came out of the brain of Charles Darwin. You remember the story of the weavers. There were ten of them. On their way they had to cross a river. When they got over, one of their number counted and found that there were only nine. Several others also counted and each found only nine. They all began to weep and lament, believing that one had been drowned, until a passer-by came and asked them what was the matter. They told him of the loss of their companion. "How many were you?" he asked. "Ten," they replied. "But you are still ten," and he counted and showed them. The trouble was that, in counting, each man had forgotten to count himself. This same blunder the materialistic philosopher has committed. He has forgotten to count himself. Yet he is the alpha. Without him who is to study nature? First he must remember himself. In every process of thought the thinker must be the beginning. And who is he? Is he dead, unconscious matter? No; he is a conscious being, and so out of consciousness all else comes.

The evolution theory, therefore, which fails to count the conscious being first is inadequate. For the materialistic philosopher, soul is merely a development of matter. Let us take their theory for granted. If it is true that consciousness has evolved out of matter, out of consciousness again must evolve an ever widening consciousness until an infinite consciousness is reached, and this infinite consciousness must first have been involved. What is the nature of consciousness? Consciousness is nearer to us then dead, unconscious matter. My nature is to live, my nature is to think and be free. But I have not yet realized this nature. The materialist will tell you that when you die, you will be extinguished; but that all that has been gained by you will exist in your progeny. If this is true, in course of time there must develop a being with such a power of will that death itself will not be able to destroy him. He will be beyond the realm of death. And when that comes he will have to be *Satchitananda*—Existence-Knowledge-Bliss Absolute. I may want to live, I may want to know, I may want to be free; yet I may die. But my progeny at some future time must realize all this; and he will exist forever, he will know all and he will be free. If he is all this, then he is God. And if God has been evolved out of matter, he must first have been involved as an all-powerful, eternal, indestructible Being; and he who has thus involved himself, must have been God Himself. He must have been the Creator, Preserver and Destroyer, for He is all-powerful. If then the final outcome is an eternal, free, all-powerful being, that being must have been involved in each one of us. As a whole this consciousness may live, but individually its duration is only for a few years. This is the conclusion of materialistic Western philosophers. Individually man dies, but as a whole, consciousness goes on until a perfect, all-powerful being results. But the perfect, all-powerful being must have been in each individual.

Now let us see what has been said in our own country. Kapila and others have regarded evolution, not as a universal fact, but as an individual fact. Each individual begins in the lowest state of consciousness and goes to the highest through the intermediate stages according to his *Karma* (sum-total of his actions), rising higher and higher through the various planes of creation. And how many individuals are there? How many souls? An infinite number, Kapila says. Matter is one, consciousness is one; but those who manifest matter and consciousness are infinite in number. This universe, as we know, is made up of variety. Then how to explain this variety, if matter is one? Nature is one, absolutely one; she is all-pervading. She is the mother of the universe and the father is the soul. Soul has no form, matter has form. The soul you cannot see, hear, taste or smell; matter you perceive, taste and smell. Whatever you can connote or denote of matter, soul is just the contrary. All souls again are similar, but not the same.

This too is the view of Sri Ramanuja (12th century A.D.), who also firmly upheld the idea of evolution (*Parinama*). He declares the soul to be eternal. Ramanuja, however, regards the soul as smaller than the smallest, while Kapila says that it is larger than the largest. Kapila also declares that all souls are one. Of this he gives a fine example. He says that just as water is one, yet entering a mango seed, a mango tree comes, or a jack-fruit seed and a jack-fruit tree comes; similarly, the soul is one, but entering different forms, it takes on different shapes and so variety arises. He describes matter as that which is limited, while spirit or soul is limitless. Soul also he describes as eternal, all-pervading, indestructible. The nature of the soul is calm, desireless. Matter, too, is desireless. Because it is dead and unconscious, it is desireless; while soul is desireless because it has no want. But if both are desireless, how can union take place? How can creation come into existence? Kapila says, creation can only come into existence by matter getting into connection with soul; and he explains it by the story of a lame man and a blind man. The lame man cannot walk, the blind man cannot see; but if the lame man climbs up on the blind man's shoulders, both can go wherever they like. So in this way, although there is no desire in matter and no desire in soul, still activity springs up when they come into union; and it is because this union has taken place that creation has come.

Now the question follows, When did the union take place? Kapila says, I see that this union has taken place and it must have come out of another union, for union has always been there and will continue; so creation must be running on eternally. But if this union is going on eternally, is it desirable for man to remain in this creation forever? Kapila replies: No, because this is an unnatural condition for him. That is why he is restless so long as he clings to the world. As, however, the soul gradually disentangles itself from the meshes of sensual pleasures, it comes to realize its natural condition. Now all the world has drunk the liquor of sensual enjoyment and has run mad—just like a drunkard who sees a dead rat and eats it, taking it for good meat. Similarly many have drunk the wine of sense pleasures and are running after the world, believing that it will make them happy. Yet they are miserable. They believe that it will give them life, yet it brings them death. If this be the case with man, how can he hanker after the infinite? Yet until he has attained infinite knowledge, he will have to be restless; for the finite is an unnatural condition for him and he must always be restless so long as he is out of his natural condition. Restlessness always indicates an unnatural condition.

Nature has been described as a beautiful young girl who fascinates the man and draws him from the right path. At first he is deceived by her, but at last he finds that nature is not to be trusted. Nature is a pot full of poison only brimmed over with a little nectar; but as soon as man finds out the poison, he runs away; and that moment the man becomes a free soul. How does man become free from nature? As soon as he discovers her deceitful character, he divorces himself from her, as it were. He says: "I will not take your food, I will not take your water. I do not want your pleasures. I wish nothing from you." Thus Kapila found out a path, following which man becomes free from nature. And what was that path? The path of going, not towards

nature, but away from nature; the old path of renunciation. "I must go away from my eyes, I must go away from
my ears, from my hands and all my organs."

Next he wanted to go away from his mind, but he
did not find this so easy. You look at the chair for one
minute; you actually perceive the chair for only one
second, the other fifty-nine seconds are in the memory.
What is the present? The present is only a point in
time. The world exists only in the present; and as the
present has no duration, the world does not really exist
except in our memory. It is therefore not difficult to
get rid of the present world, but it is exceedingly difficult to get rid of the past and future worlds. However,
in course of time man will be able to put down the
mental world and then will come perfect calmness,
which is his true nature.

The difference between Kapila's evolution and Western evolution is that while Western evolution is a universal evolution and imperfectly worked out, Kapila's
evolution is individual and perfectly worked out. Kapila
says: This world is a dangerous place. Man must try to
escape from it. So he preaches, Give up; there is no
happiness here. Evolution here is not evolution, it is
really revolution. Like the bullock tied to the oil-press,
who may walk nine or ten miles a day, yet does not
go away from the oil-press, but always remains in the
same room; so we remain tied to nature in the same
way. We may be born again and again, but always
are we led away by the same attraction to the sense;
always the same lust enslaves us.

In nature, therefore, we find things, not progressing,
but going in a circle. In creation it is never evolution,
but always revolution;—January, February, March and

again at the end of twelve months, January, February, March; summer, autumn, winter and spring, and once more summer and autumn; boyhood, youth, old age, and again babyhood, boyhood, etc. It is all a *Samsara-chakra* (wheel of earthly life), an eternal going round and round in a circle. The only evolution is inside yourself. The more you go within, the more you grow strong.

So if you want to have real evolution, real power, you must go inside yourself. The moment you go outside, you dissipate yourself, you scatter your forces. For this reason, Kapila says: Give up this world which is always drawing you outward. Have no smell even of the world about you. Then alone you will realize your highest nature. And as soon as you realize it, there will be no motion for you, for you will know yourself to be all-pervading; and if you are all-pervading, you are everywhere, you cannot move. Then you will understand the meaning of *Shantih* or final beatitude.

Thus Kapila has worked out his theory until it has become a fact. The western theory is still only a theory, because it has not been carried to a final conclusion. Beyond Kapila, however, stands monism. According to monism there is no such thing as evolution. Monism says there is only one; there is none else besides myself. Hence evolution is all the trick of *Maya* (delusion or unreality). The whole of this development is only imagination. If you are infinite and perfect, how can you develop? And you are infinite, you are perfect and you are only one. You may be imagining yourself as finite, that does not matter; you may be imagining yourself as many, that too does not matter. Sri Ramakrishna used to say that a flint stone may stay thousands of years under water, but when it is taken out and struck, the spark will still come out. So you may have been living in Maya for ages and ages, yet that does not change the fact that you are really infinite and perfect. No evolution therefore can exist in a world of reality. In a false world it exists, but nowhere else. Evolution means Maya, means illusion. You have never been evolving. You have been dreaming a big dream for ages and when you wake up, you are at once a Buddha. Then you will know that you have never evolved, that growth or change are impossible for you.

Now let us imagine the three theories. According to Western philosophers evolution has been going on in nature from the beginning. According to Kapila, evolution is in the mind only. And according to monism, there is no evolution at all. You are perfect, you cannot evolve. It is all a chakram (a wheel) like the bullock tied to the oil mill; and when illumination comes, you will realize that all was a dream. According to the monistic standpoint, there is no progress, no diversion. As one wave of the ocean rises and falls and then another rises, but the ocean remains the same; so the waves of creation rise and fall.

If, however, we look at the world from our present limited standpoint, I think Kapila's theory the most perfect of all. You know that in India philosophy is not a theory. When a man writes out a Dharsana (philosophical system), he does not write a theory, but what he has realized, what he has seen; so what he gives is a fact, not a theory. Hence if, with Kapila, you believe in two entities, then Kapila's explanation is the best of all explanations. We must evolve as individuals and the final end of all evolution is to realize that we are infinite and not finite.

REBIRTH AND EVOLUTION
By *Swami Paramananda*

The complex nature of our existence always demands explanation and in seeking to find it, man has been led to investigate both the physical and spiritual realms, for the study of life is the most interesting of all study. The very fact that we exist makes us want to understand the process of life:—how and whence we have come into existence and what happens after death. The discovery of the theory of evolution by modern science led many to believe that it would solve the whole problem of life. But the theory as presented in the West does not offer the explanation we require. Western scientists say that the natural struggle for existence must lead every germ of life to progress and that it cannot stop evolving until it has developed the power to resist all difficulties; that, by the law of the survival of the fittest, wherever there is a necessity of escaping from greater forces, the lesser forces are striving to acquire greater power; hence every living thing, from the minutest insect up, is constantly compelled by its inherent nature to try to evolve its life-force. They also attempt to show how the body evolves through the lower stages and continues to evolve until it is perfected. But the explanation of modern physical evolution can never fully satisfy us, for it does not account for the higher planes of manifestation.

This, however, is not the case with the ancient evolutionists of India, like Kapila, who lived in the seventh century B.C. and who extended his conception beyond the physical to moral and spiritual evolution. These early Seers realized that there can be no evolution without involution. The fact that something cannot come out of nothing, as modern science also affirms, proves that involution must precede evolution. The relation, indeed, between evolution and involution is as inseparable as between cause and effect; and just as to understand the effect we must know the cause, so to understand our present state of evolution we must know all that has gone before; for what we call our mental and physical inheritances are not matters of chance, but the direct outcome of our past. The wise ones who have been brave and strong enough to lift the veil, know that this life cannot be explained until we connect it with a previous existence and that the future existence will find its explanation in the present one; for the law of life is nothing but the process of evolution. When we grasp this, we are able to comprehend more clearly the diversity and inequality apparent everywhere. Why are not all men alike? Does an All-mighty, All-merciful Lord create one happy and another miserable? What brings the distinction? There must be some cause, for there can be no effect without a cause, and the inequalities in outer condition and mental power among human beings are effects of causes which lie imbedded in the character of each individual.

The gross is not all. There is another known as the subtle body, which is composed of finer and less destructible material. This subtle body consists of mind, intellect and the sense of "I". In it are stored up all the impressions gathered through our different lives. Only by knowing this subtler part of man, wherein dwells the individuality, can we gain insight into the course of his evolution, and understand why his life varies from every other. We create for ourselves these differences, either consciously or unconsciously. Our destiny is not governed, as we imagine, by a supernatural power. The happiness and misery which we experience here are not forced upon us by an arbitrary Providence, but are the inevitable result of our own thoughts and deeds. We must reap what we have sown. No one can give us what we do not deserve, nor can any one keep from us the blessing we have earned. We ourselves have the power to make and unmake our destiny. Therefore if we are born with certain defects in our character, if we are placed in an unhappy environment, although these are due to our own past errors, such conditions are by no means unalterable, but can be counteracted by our present mode of living. When, however, a person dies without completing his task in life, with his goal unattained, is everything ended for him? Has he no further chance? Sri Krishna answers in the Bhagavad-Gita: "There is no loss for him either here or hereafter; for he who doesth good never attaineth an evil condition. In his new birth he regaineth the knowledge acquired in his former incarnations and striveth again for his end. He is irresistibly led by his previous tendencies. Thus purified by many births and rebirths, he reacheth the Supreme Goal."

Now the question naturally arises: If we existed before, why is it that we do not remember? We do not recall many things that took place in our childhood, yet we cannot say that we did not exist then. Our memory is not in its pure state, our mind at present is not collected or focused enough to penetrate the past, therefore our knowledge is limited and our recollection vague. Also the power of memory varies. There are some people who can recall even the smallest detail of their childhood; and there are others who do not remember what happened a year ago, or even yesterday. This shows how minds differ. The memory, however, can be purified, as we find in the lives of the Great Ones. Buddha, for instance, remembered his past; and many Yogis who lead lives of contemplation and absolute purity also are able to know their previous births, for the mind becomes like a crystal and reflects everything clearly. Mind is the cause of our bondage and mind is the cause of our freedom. It is the unfulfilled desires of the mind which impel us to seek embodiment in order to satisfy them. Desires are like the seeds of new births and the character of those desires shapes our future. We read in the Gita: "Whatever state of being a man dwelleth upon at the time of leaving the body, that verily he attaineth." In other words he attains the condition he has most constantly held in his thought through this lifetime. This means that a man cannot gain anything other than what he has created for himself by his habits of mind. He may wish to have something else, but his own nature, formed by his voluntary or involuntary thoughts and deeds, will impel him to move in a certain direction. If we wish to change our present course, we must cultivate such habits of thought as will counteract the past and carry us in a new direction.

What do we really want? Do we want things which are temporary or things which are lasting? Can we be satisfied to go on through this round of birth and death, finding little gratifications for this one span of life, identifying ourselves with mere bodily existence, seeking nothing beyond? If we long for something else, we must work for it. We must unfold all our latent powers. We must learn to know our true nature. Through moral evolution alone man can attain his freedom. We can gain material blessings by striving for material things; for whatever a man constantly thinks of and works for, he gains. But until he can unfold his moral and spiritual nature, that nature within him which is mighty, imperishable, he cannot be free. Life is indestructible. All the great philosophers and sages recognize that life has not its rising and setting in this one small existence. It has been and will be. The fullness of evolution could not be reached during one embodiment, for the time is not long enough. The soul has not finished its experience; it has not gathered all the knowledge it requires and therefore it must return to gather more. "Why should I not come back as often as I am capable of acquiring fresh knowledge, fresh experience? Do I bring away so much from once that there is nothing to repay the trouble of coming back?" the great German writer Lessing exclaims. And Huxley says: "Like the doctrine of evolution itself, that of transmigration has its roots in the realm of reality. None but hasty thinkers will reject it on the ground of inherent absurdity."

The doctrine of evolution and reincarnation explains the law of life; and when we understand it, we have no feeling of bitterness towards our present conditions. A rebellious spirit will never help us escape from suffering and ignorance; only work with understanding can free us. When we learn to mould this life of ours wisely, then we regard it as a privilege and a blessing to possess it, because through it we can manifest the glory of Godhood. This is the purpose of evolution. Every germ of life is descended from the Almighty and every germ must ultimately attain union with its Source. Most people are at present making the journey unconsciously, fettered by many desires which can never be satisfied. To try to fulfill them is like adding fuel to fire. At every step we must use discrimination. We must question what we want and what can give us what we want. We must also bear in mind that this life of ours is not a matter of accident; that it is not so temporary or so limited as we imagine; but that it is everlasting.

Faith in the eternity of our existence will lift us above the plane of physical consciousness to a plane where we shall gain the power to live our lives nobly and fulfill all our duties wisely. Man does not fear to live when he understands what life is. He does not wish to run away then, for who runs away from life? Do you suppose that people who commit suicide do so because they do not love life? No. It is the bondage, the ignorance, the miseries of life from which they wish to escape; but they take the wrong road. They destroy the instrument with which they might unfold their nature and gain that which would bring them what their soul is really craving. No living being hates life or wishes to escape from it. It is from death we want to escape; and this last enemy, death, can never be overcome until we have evolved our spiritual nature, the nature which is undying, free and complete. Infinity has no lack; and when limited man finds his unlimited nature—that which is part of God, then he casts off all bondage and transcends the realm of death.

The idea of reincarnation takes from us all sense of impatience and injustice, because it shows that we are not put here arbitrarily, with only a few years in which to do all that we have to do; but that we shall be given other opportunities to work out our desires and find fullness of life; that what we have left unfinished we shall have another chance to finish. The majority of people, who live under slavery to their lower desires, have no choice as to the environment and conditions of their new birth. They have created a chain, a weight which holds them down; but it is a self-created fetter, which they themselves can break by purifying their desires and elevating their thoughts.

Every mortal must be awakened some day or other to his spiritual nature. It may come gradually through the natural process of evolution, or suddenly through disappointment and suffering. Therefore we must not imagine that all the suffering we see in human life is a curse. Great blessings sometimes come through pain or grief, and a man who understands the law does not cry out against his fate. He lives here with serenity. He knows that nothing happens without a definite purpose; that the experiences of pleasure and pain, of success or failure, which a man undergoes, all help him to evolve his higher nature and lead him to ultimate perfection. Therefore let each one of us live his life consciously and cheerfully. Let us never give way to despair or look upon this life as a burden. Let us work with perseverance and undepressed heart until we realize that for our true Self there is no death, but that this life of ours is a part of the Infinite, Indestructible and All-pervading Life.

HISTORY OF REINCARNATION
By *Sister Daya*

T he idea of reincarnation or rebirth is not associated with any one race or epoch, it is coincident with the history of human reason. Of this ancient concept James Freeman Clarke writes in his "Ten Great Religions,"—"It" (reincarnation) "was taught by three great religions, that of Egypt, of Brahmanism, and of Buddhism; by Pythagoras, Empedocles, and Plato among Greek philosophers; by the Neo-Platonists, the Jewish Kabala, and the Arab philosophers; by Origen and other church fathers; by the Gnostics, the Manichaeans, the Druids; and in recent times by Fourier and others."

Let us go as far back as possible in human tradition and discover if we can the earliest mention of this theory of spiritual evolution. Although there are many discussions as to the priority of this Bible or that, it is safe to assume that the Vedas of India are sufficiently ancient to be ranked among the first of holy books. At any rate they are the oldest Aryan heritage that we have. The date of the Vedas is given as about 2000 B.C. These Scriptures consist chiefly of childlike hymns in worship of nature. They are songs of praise almost entirely—but they are vibrant with the sense of endless manifesting life and consciousness, which later developed into the grand

51

and more organized concept of the soul's round of births and deaths as it is set forth in the Upanishads, the Bhagavad-Gita, and in practically all the great Indian epics and Scriptures. In fact reincarnation is the very warp and woof of Hindu life, socially, philosophically and spiritually. As the oldest sacred books refer all their knowledge to a teaching infinitely more remote, it is fair to assume that it was an ancient idea with the Vedic *Rishis*.

Egypt comes next in our consideration. Herodotus states that "the Egyptians are the first who propounded the theory that the human soul is imperishable and that where the body of any one dies it enters into some other creature that may be ready to receive it, and that when it has gone the round of all created forms on land, in water and in air, then it once more enters a human body born for it; and that this cycle of existence for the soul takes place in three thousand years." He likewise says that "some of the Greeks adopted this opinion, some earlier, others later, as if it were their own." Egypt undoubtedly must have had a very profound philosophy to have held such minds as that of Pythagoras for instance, who spent many years in Egypt delving into her deepest mysteries. But today we lack the key which would unlock for us these mysteries so jealously guarded by her priests. As a result her religion appears to us confused and often grotesque, while her idea of rebirth through animal and other forms seems a perversion of the pure Indo-Aryan concept. The true wisdom of Egypt is often conveyed to us by the Greeks who came under its influence, notably Pythagoras. He likewise seemed to teach the descent of the soul into the bodies of beasts. But this is declared by some of his later followers to be merely symbolic.

Plato's great name has always been associated with the idea of rebirth. Aristotle also makes reference to it. Nemesius emphatically declared that all the Greeks who believed in immortality believed also in reincarnation. Greece was constantly in touch with Oriental thought and receptive to its influence. Thus Neo-Platonism which arose around the first century and was contemporary with the Alexandrian Gnostics, sought to combine the doctrines of Pythagoras, Plato and Buddhism. Ammonius Saccas, Plotinus and Porphyry in the third century, Iamblichus in the fourth, Hierocles and Proclus in the fifth and Damascius in the sixth were among the great Neo-Platonists, who helped establish the idea of reincarnation in the West. The Alexandrian Gnostics likewise taught it. They sought to furnish young Christianity with an adequate philosophy and echoes of their influence sound through the Fourth Gospel. Christianity was most powerfully affected by these ancient ideas. Especially did reincarnation cause her disquietude. It was too reminiscent of the pagan world. Origen and many of the early church fathers held to it. Origen's master, Clemens Alexandrinus taught it as a divine tradition, authorized by St. Paul himself. Ruffinus in his letter to Anastasius says that "This opinion was common among the primitive fathers." Heretical sects such as the Manichaeans, were rife with it and handed it down to medieval times where it was perpetuated in the teachings of the Bogomites, Paulicians, Priscillians, and many others. Mr. Walker in his book on "Reincarnation" states

that "It was an essential part of church philosophy
for many centuries in the rank and file of Christian thought." Its prevalence can be gauged by the
fact that at the Council of Constantinople about 550
A.D. the Church pronounced it Anathema.

That there must have been a strong Hebrew influence upholding it is more than likely although it
does not seem to be included in the Old Testament.
Some of the Apocryphal books refer to it as does
the Talmud and the Kabala. The Jewish Therapeutae
of Egypt and the Essenes of Palestine from whom
some claim Christ received His early teaching, were
imbued with it. There is nothing in the New Testament opposed to it and certain statements of the
Christ Himself more than implied it, showing it to
be a prevailing tenet of the day. There is little question that Persian thought added its stream of influence to those streams flowing in from Greece,
Egypt and India. The Magi, so intimately connected
with the birth of Christianity, brought it as one of
their gifts.

But because of church bigotry on the one hand
and materialism on the other, the Christian West
seems to have dropped the idea of the soul's evolution, without which its much vaunted physical evolution is an empty husk. But this is only "officially
speaking." It would take many pages to recount the
utterances of occidental thinkers, upholding the idea
of rebirth. Italy of the middle ages had her voices
which proclaimed it. Giordano Bruno's for example.
Many sects and societies secretly held it. The trou-
badours and mimes are thought by many to have
conveyed under romantic imagery the most profound

truths of the human soul.

The German philosophers gave it their serious attention: Schopenhauer, Lessing, Hegel, Leibnitz, Herder, and Fichte the younger. Richard Wagner long had it in mind to write a great opera around the theme of Buddhism, while the Scandinavian mythology from which the legends of "The Ring" are derived included metampsychosis or reincarnation. Jacob Boehme, Swedenborg, Paracelsus and other great mystics adhered to it. The Cambridge Platonists, conspicuously Henry More, spoke for it. It captivated Fourier and Leroux. Poets and fiction writers have used it as a theme and many refer to their belief in it. Even in the modern church it has had its defenders. Bishops in England and Ireland have not hesitated to promulgate it. Especially since modern means of transportation have brought about closer contact with the Orient, has this age-old conception renewed its hold on our imaginations. It has been recently calculated that among the orthodox movements in this country, such as Theosophy, New Thought, etc., there are at least 12,000,000 followers, and of these very many hold to the idea of reincarnation. In fact in the world today the majority of the human race believe in it. All the countries which have welcomed Buddhism, such as Ceylon, Burma, Java, China, Japan, Tibet, Central Asia, Siberia and even Swedish Lapland, come under its influence. The primitive heart and the philosophic mind find equal satisfaction in it. It encircles the world and has left its traces everywhere. It is making belief in immortality again possible for the skeptical West. As the materialistic philosopher Hume states in his essay on "The Immortality of the Soul": "The soul, therefore, if immortal existed before our birth, and if the former existence noways concerns us, neither will the latter. Metempsychosis is, therefore, the only system of this kind that philosophy can harken to."

THE GREAT LAW OF JUSTICE
By Swami Paramananda

he word *Karma* is derived from the Sanskrit root *kri* meaning work, or that
activity which is produced as the result
of action and reaction. *Karma*, therefore, literally
means the Law of cause and effect; not only cause
and effect as it is manifested on the physical, phenomenal plane, but that which goes deep down to the
root of our being. There are certain results which we
reap in the form of suffering or enjoyment for ourselves or for others that we are not able to account
for by outer circumstance. The only way we can find
any explanation for them is to go beneath the surface
life around us and realize that what is happening today is the outcome of yesterday,—is rooted in some
past cause. The definition of this Law of cause and
effect we find very clearly given by Manu, the great
Law-giver of India, who is also called "The Father of
Man": "Thou canst not gather what thou dost not
sow; as thou dost plant the seed so will it grow." Later
on we find an echo of this in St. Paul when he says:
"Whatsoever a man soweth that shall he also reap";
and I do not doubt that as we go back into the Old
Testament, the Egyptian Scriptures, the Chinese and
other ancient classics, we shall find the same principle
given, because it is a Law and not merely a dogmatic

assertion. It is the Law upon which the whole of human destiny is established. In India it is known as the Law of *Karma* by which a man reaps only as he sows.

Today many among us are rebellious; we feel that there is a great deal of divine injustice in the world. Let me read to you, however, what Max Muller, one of the greatest of Orientalists, has to say on this subject: "Indian philosophy contains no outcry against divine injustice, and in no way encourages suicidal expedients. They would, in fact, be of no avail, because according to Indian views, the same troubles and the same problems would have to be faced again and again in another life. Considering that the aim of all Indian philosophy was the removal of suffering, which was caused by nescience, and the attainment of the highest happiness which was produced by knowledge, we should have more right to call it endaemonistic than pessimistic." Perhaps you will not care to accept a law like this which prevents a man escaping from his miseries even by bodily death. Yet what kind of justice would there be in this universe if those who have done great harm to others could evade all consequences merely by taking their own lives? We would not want to live in a universe whose constitution was as vulnerable as that. Do not think, however, that this great Law is adamantine. By means of it we create, but what we create we also have power to destroy; through it we make and we can unmake. If our present life is the sum total of our past thoughts, actions and desires, then certainly it stands to reason that we can change it—we can re-create our life, and that is better than to try to get rid of it.

There are some people who look upon *Karma* as

though it were fate. They say, "It is my *Karma*, it is my doom." In India, however, the wise man does not take it that way. If such a person is placed in the midst of hardship he knows how to overcome his difficulties, how to dispel the clouds and enjoy once more the clear sky and the sunshine. We can counteract,—that is the secret. By our prayers, our aspirations, our power of service, in fact by means of the vitality God has given to us, we can so transmute our thoughts and emotions that they help us to balance our past. Certain individuals have an idea that it does not make any difference what they think or do here and now, that so long as they subscribe to some religion or belong to some creed, they will have their salvation. Practical wisdom, however, shows us that salvation has nothing to do with dogma, doctrine or anything of that kind. Salvation comes through following a fundamental principle of life. Only thus do we advance. If we find ourselves handicapped, we should not feel thwarted, we should not feel that it is our fate,—something forced upon us. We can outgrow these conditions, we can transcend them. How soon? That depends upon the intensity we put into our efforts, upon our earnestness, our zeal, our sincerity of purpose; according to these, we overcome.

Does not this furnish a logical basis for life? Without it we find that there is nothing but injustice. We see a child, blind, deaf or a cripple, while side by side with him, perhaps in the same family, is one who is born a genius,—a scientist, poet or musician,—and we ask why this should be. At first we may seek to explain it on the grounds of heredity, but often we

fail to find any connecting hereditary links. The orthodox will try to give a solution by saying that it
is the will of God. But God is all-loving. We can
imagine that almighty Providence through His will
bestowing blessing upon His children, but we cannot think of Him cursing any one. There is, however, the eternal Law, "as a man soweth, so shall he
reap," and this gives us the key.

The whole index of a man's life is contained in
his soul. He may conceive a crime in a cave or a
jungle; he may commit it in a dark corner, and no
one may see him do it, yet he knows and is tor-
mented by it. Sometimes he is so burdened by the
knowledge of it that he seeks to rid himself of
it by confessing it. How do we explain this if he
does not carry the Law within himself, if he is not
the creator of his own destiny? It is not that some
divine Providence is holding a rod over us and is
taking account of everything that we think and do.
Suppose through misguided zeal we have done
something which we regret, we also have the power
to undo it. It will not help matters to sit in a corner and say, "I have sinned, my life is doomed." The
thing is to get up with courage and determination
and make a fresh start. Determination is half the
battle. In this way we counteract our error. It is one
of the things we need to teach children,—also grown-
up people,—those who are discontent, who are
always finding fault with their lot, with their fellow-
beings, with their superiors, with everything around
them.

The destiny of man is in great measure controlled by himself; no one else can make us think right,

and certainly if we do not think in the right way, we cannot act in the right way. It is like sowing seeds. Lord Buddha, the great compassionate teacher of India, gives a very interesting and graphic picture of this whole process when he says: "If a man speaks or acts with evil thought, pain will follow him, as the wheel follows the foot of the ox that draws the carriage." Likewise if a man does anything with good intent, with loving heart, happiness follows him with the same precision. Why not choose the path of happiness? There is no one who is asking us to be unkind; there is no one who is asking us to sow on the field of life poisonous seeds. We may say that we sow them accidentally, that we were angry, or spoke an unkind word by chance. Do not let us take any such chance with our spiritual life, then accidents like this will not happen.

I always compare this life of ours with a harvest field. The man who is industrious, who is diligent, who is careful, he does not take any chances with his harvest. He tills the soil, and then he carefully sows the seed, but he does not think that his duty ends there,—he keeps it watered and watches over it until there comes the time of harvesting. We may think that we do not have to do any of these things. Perhaps our neighbor's harvest is going to suffice for us, or some one may be kind enough to share with us. There is, however, no real satisfaction or surety in this. We must, every one of us, make our own life abundant, and we can do it, we have the power to do it. God has given us hands and mind and brain and heart. With these we can work and counteract any handicap which may arise against us.

The Great Law is not just a relentless machine. It is something that we can use, that we can operate with intelligence, and it will give us tremendous impetus for advance in every step of our life. Take the law of love,—love has tremendous healing. If a man thinks of love and acts with loving interest, if he constantly meditates on love, he will be healed and he will help to bring healing to the world. Think of the miracles that are performed through love! We know these principles, yet if we do not apply them how can we expect to reap the harvest? That is the question. As a man soweth in his heart and through his deed, so must he reap. The Law is very simple. You may say, "We sometimes find a good person suffering and an innocent person unjustly accused." We do not always see the Law's fulfillment. Even suffering has its blessing and I do not say this with any morbid sense. Life has tremendous lessons for us all, but we have to be wide awake to learn these lessons. Condemnation, bitterness, discord, rebellion, these are not going to solve our problems. We must believe in our destiny, we must believe that it is not something vague and indefinite, but that it is in our own keeping, the exact result of our thoughts and actions.

There is nothing that can check our progress unless we ourselves step in our own light. Try to understand the theory of it, the logic of it. Something cannot come out of nothing. This is one of the greatest points in Hindu philosophy and religion, logic and ethics, a point the Hindus discovered a long, long time ago. Instead of trying to throw the blame on Providence, they arrived at this great Law of cause and effect. Evolution cannot take place without involution. Carlyle gives us a similar conception. "The curtains of yesterday drop down, the curtains of to-morrow roll up; but yesterday and tomorrow both are. Believe what thou findest written in the sanctuaries of man's soul, even as all thinkers, in all ages have devoutly read it there." This life, as we find it, with all its endless advantages and disadvantages, oppor-tunities and the lack of them, is not the result of accident, but only as we are able to make our con-nection with yesterday can we find an explanation for today.

Those who understand the Law never waste any time. They know that all the energy, service, intelli-gent effort which they put into life, they will reap in full measure. It cannot be otherwise. Life is not for idling. It does not do to take a lethargic attitude towards our destiny, and expect some miraculous happening to bring us good fortune over night. The man of genius keeps on working. Those who grasp the true meaning of *Karma*—of cause and effect—they do not sit and weep when ill-fortune comes, they try to counteract it by doing something good. Evil is always counteracted by good. That is the eternal law. Lord Buddha told his disciples: "Hatred is never conquered by hatred, hatred is conquered by love." Since our pain and suffering and sorrow are the results of past hatred, misguided zeal, and misdeeds, what we need to do is to direct our forces properly along the lines of love, wisdom, and service. No matter how we are born, or where we are placed, we can change the whole current of our destiny. Such is the Law of *Karma*. It is not fate. It gives us the explanation why certain things are happening, and wherefrom they

come, even though we may not see the process actually take place before our eyes. It reveals to us in a
very interesting way our great responsibility.

A man's past life explains his temperament, his
tendencies, and his opportunities or lack of them in
this life. Suppose we have some limitations, what are
we to do? Strive to overcome them by right thought
and action. This should be one of the fundamental
principles in education. Instead of bringing children
up to think that they must either endure with a morbid spirit of suffering, or else react with passion, they
should be taught to keep on working, so that through
their work, through their service, through their intelligent operation of life itself, they may be able to wipe
out past ills and build their life and destiny on a new
basis. In this way they redeem themselves and they
redeem others. We have so much that we can share
with others. That is the way the Law of *Karma* works.
Whatever we gain, we have done something to earn
it. There is no chance, no accident in this cosmic
universe. There cannot be, because it is controlled
by a great, unfailing, all-loving and all-just Intelligence. So long as we have any complaint, any spirit
of discontent, it means we do not understand.

If a man places himself in the path of an engine,
he will be crushed and all his strength will not avail
against it. In the same way, it is only a foolhardy
person who tries to go against the Law. One who
understands the operation of the Law, he uses that
great power intelligently, and he accomplishes
great things. The Law of *Karma* is very much like fire.
Fire cooks our food and also it can cause disaster. A
child out of fascination for the flames may put his

hand into it and be burned. Yet we cannot say fire is evil. A thing that gives us benefit also can become detrimental if we do not know how to handle it. That is the idea of Law. If we oppose it, it may hurt us and hinder us, but if we know how to work with it, it will always help us.

It is not, however, merely through logic that we can remind ourselves that we must do this and we must not do that, and if we do this, we are going to reap that. We must lift our mind to a higher level where these conditions can no longer bind us. In the presence of light all darkness vanishes. Leave your world of sorrow, and misery, and turbulence, and struggle, and seek to rise to that plane of consciousness which mystics and sages and all spiritual beings define as Light. If troubles and difficulties are hurled upon you, do not try to find escape by ordinary means. Go within your own self. Retire within the cave of your heart, as the Hindus call it. There nothing can ever touch you, there you will find your security and there you will be made whole. Christ speaks of it as entering into the closet and shutting the doors; Lord Buddha refers to it as that "Island of Peace," where no storm can reach, that "Island of Rest," where no turbulence can come, no disturbance touch you. Yet how many of us seek this refuge? If someone strikes us, or unjustly accuses us, we think that we must do him even greater harm in order to get even with him. This however, is not in accordance with the Law of our spiritual being. If we indulge in hatred and bitterness, we are merely sowing poisonous seeds on the field of life, and we shall have to reap the harvest.

Let us rather sow the seeds which will blossom forth with fragrant flowers and bear luscious fruits. The field,—this human field—is allotted to us, and we all have our choice. Our hands, our brain, our heart are given to us for inspiration, in order that we may produce something of value. We want happiness, we want pleasure, we want God's blessing. Every one of us would like to have the ability of the genius, the peace of the saint, the vision of the wise man, but we forget that they do not acquire these qualities accidentally. They work for them, they live for them, and they die for them. Most of you will say, "We have heard this before,—it is not anything new." That is true. There is nothing new, and there is no need for anything new. We have not even tried to put into practice all the beneficent, beautiful principles that already have been given to us for the upbuilding of our individual life and the life of the whole. It is for us with determination to apply these principles; to put them to the test of science and of practical living. The Law of cause and effect will stand the test of science. Go and think in the right rhythm and you will find that you have generated a force within yourself, have created a dynamo of invincible power which can reconstruct your life; and above all remember,— hatred is never conquered by hatred; evil is never conquered by evil, it is conquered only by good,—it is healed by the influx of life and love.

THE THREE WORLDS
by Sister Devamata

lthough in the West we talk more frequently of two worlds, the here and the hereafter, we are compelled to recognize scientifically that there must be three worlds. The future presupposes a past, and as a matter of fact, the present is only the point where past and future meet. We know that if there is a heaven there must be some state known as hell; and that point where they meet is our earthly realm. We read in the Eastern scriptures of men who conquered the three worlds; and in the Bhagavad-Gita Sri Krishna says, "There is nothing for Me to accomplish. Naught is there in the three worlds unattained or to be attained by Me."

What are the three worlds? To the gross ignorant mind they are really worlds, three distinct places. Those who do not recognize reincarnation think that when we leave our earthly existence we go to either of two worlds—one we call heaven the other hell. Many forms of theology are based upon man's trying to free himself from hell; thus his whole effort is directed toward enabling him to go to that place where he may have everything he has not had here.

As a matter of fact, however, man lives in three worlds every moment. The human soul stands, as it were, in its present embodiment, like a longitudinal section of the entire universe. In man at this moment lies the whole history of all the worlds. Just as he passes through the complete history of evolution in the prenatal state, so all during his life he is rising and falling between these worlds, repeating over and over again each age of ascent and descent, up and down that sliding scale. The wise man is he who concentrates his whole realization in the now, in the present moment. He does not wait for some tomorrow to make a change of condition which will reveal to him a new world. He sets out to study and philosophize today; to live and choose his worlds here and now; to determine in what realm he will exist, on what plane he will think and act, what he will manifest, for at every moment there is, in every germ, in every atom, the possibility of manifesting in one or all of the states or worlds. These three worlds correspond to what is known in Hindu philosophy as the qualities of nature, the three *gunas: tamas,* the dark and dull; *rajas,* the excessively active, and *sattva,* the pure and serene.

When man first awakens from the brute state which we call *tamas,* he finds himself heavy, dull, like one who is just waking from a sleep. Imagine someone who has plunged down into the depths of some sticky, thick substance like molasses and has been trying to rise and escape. As he comes to the surface how clogged up he must feel by that which has held him back! So are we when we awaken from this sleep of matter. Up until this point we live in the lowest realm, covered over by the material of the universe. We think that we are awake because we are aware of our striving to acquire more and more of material things. But so long as man seeks in that lowest realm he is still asleep, still in the brute stage. As long as the material things seem to be realities he is in the state of *tamas*; he is heavy and dull and cannot rise.

What can be done about it? When one wishes to rouse himself after a night's sleep he moves about and does all he can to cause the body to become active. Even so must we work with ourselves when we waken from the sleep of matter and begin to discover the other worlds. Very few people are living even in the human or middle world today, for this second world is the moral world and man's moral sense for the most part has not yet been awakened. It seems a terrible thing that our whole economic fabric continues to be based on voluntary dishonesty though we know this dishonesty as an actual fact. Most large fortunes have not been gained by pure honesty; the very fact that the gain has been based on pushing others aside or on the survival of the fittest shows that it is not a moral act. Therefore, everyone who is living this sort of life is still on the brute plane. Whenever we are led to do any one thing to gain for ourself at the cost of someone else we remain on the lower plane.

If we once recognize, however, that honesty is of greater value than the prize we are tempted to steal, the temptation ceases because the jewel of honesty means more to us. If the inner beauty has greater reality for us than the outer we will not be enticed to belittle ourself at its cost. Those who have placed too much value on material things must recognize, sooner or later, that they are living in the lowest realm, that realm which we call hell and which is a state of ignorance and egotism. The only thing in the world that can make us suffer is ourselves. It is the ego that creates all the hell that we can suffer. By a selfish act we may seem to gain today, but we have set ourselves at odds with every other self in the universe, and that whole army of selves is going to battle against us.

Go out into the world of competition and ask any man if he enjoys it. He may think that it is a pleasure for a time, just for the exhilaration of the game, but how quickly he grows weary! Look at the businessmen of today; see if they are happy. Perhaps a sudden turn of value elates them for a moment; then comes another turn and they go bent with burdens. Why? Because they are living in the lowest realm. Nobody can be happy there. As long as we have any material ambition, as long as we set up any golden calf to worship, whether it is wealth, health, name, fame or power—anything that represents a return here and now in this material world—we are living in the lowest realm. We need never expect to be happy there. We can stay there as long as we wish, as long as the game amuses us, but we will never find happiness there, because we are in a state of constant anxiety lest someone should rob us. This is what hell is and to a great extent we are living in it now.

How can we get out of it? By just being human beings, and not following our brute instincts. It is the instinct of the brute to snatch the bone from another animal; it is the instinct of the brute to scratch the one who hurts it. It is the instinct of the brute to kill, to fight. Are we going to permit such inclinations to be ours? If they arise in our hearts even in the subtlest form—a resentment against conditions; a feeling that "this is my right and I will fight for it"—we are snatching at the bone; we still have our feet down in the lowest realm.

The human state is preeminently the moral state. If we wish to live in the middle realm, called by the Hindus, *rajas*, our standard of action must always be the moral standard. It cannot be, "Will I lose so many dollars" but rather, "Will I lose my moral conviction? Will my sense of fairness be dulled?" When we come to the point where money, time, strength and good opinion count as nothing beside the sense of moral uprightness, then we may know we have evolved into human beings and that is what is expected of us.

The middle plane is the plane of character. It is for the development of man's higher moral consciousness, for the education of the moral being. If we have lifted ourselves to this plane we must continue to put the moral law into practice, for every day that we choose the lower rather than the higher, the false rather than the true, we keep ourselves just so much longer in a state of ignorance, *tamas*. Do not imagine that wealth, health or popularity can ever bring man the least glory in the sight of God. What does the greatest emperor in the world count beside a Buddha or a Christ? Even in our own community, what does learning count beside a man of character? Who are those who stand out? A man towers above others, not because of his education, not because of any worldly power or advantage that he may have, but because he is a man of perfect moral character. We must realize this, for it is of genuine value to us: The power of distinguishing between right and wrong, real and unreal is the only knowledge that will stand as true when we become awakened. If our standards are false it is because we are still in the lower realm; if we pay court to men of money rather than to men of character it is because we have not risen even to the middle realm.

We need not be proud of a civilization that is based on machines and material achievements. This simply means that it is the culmination of the brute state—the state of matter. We may consider giving working men more and more wages, but every day the standard of morality is going down. Look back to the days when perfection counted, when a master carpenter or shoemaker was an honored person in his community. He did not think whether he was going to earn ten dollars a day or not; he was more concerned about producing a good piece of furniture or a well-made pair of shoes. He had a sense of pride in the quality of his work. Do you think that even if he was poor he was less happy than the man today who is glad to cheat in every way to get ten dollars without working for it? And yet this is what is happening. Everyone is striking for higher wages, but no one is striking for personal efficiency. Why? Because matter is weighing us down, pushing us back into the realm of the brute. We should blush for our civilization, for anything that is so false. And when we do want to start something better, what is it? In order to level all these conditions we suggest, "You have so much money; give half of it to me, and it will better the state of the world." But does anyone talk of the leveling of character, not by pushing it all down, but by pulling it all up? We must value our character, our efficiency, our moral standard far above everything else. We should prefer to walk in the plainest of clothes, poor, even despised by others in order to keep ourselves pure and free from the lower world; if we do not then we have no right to live anywhere except in that realm.

Why is it, if poverty is so unpleasant, that those who have awakened to higher ideals choose it? If we recognize the fact that the man who has had to make his own way, who has had to struggle, is the better man in the long run, why then do we consider struggle such a misfortune? We give false standards to the world. The possession of money is not the source of happiness. It is that awareness of the majesty, the privilege, the glory of being a human being, not merely in body, but human in mind, in heart, in the moral consciousness. And if we would rise up out of this middle realm into that highest one which few have entered we must first go step by step up the moral ladder.

Living in the middle realm, even at the top-most point, is not all of our duty. But do not imagine that we can even begin to be spiritual until we have learned to be absolutely upright in all our dealings; until we have learned to observe the strictest purity within and without; until we have become absolutely truthful in every word and thought and have learned to shrink from injuring the least of God's creatures. Only when we refuse to advance ourselves at the cost of the smallest or humblest of His children can we hope for spiritual vision. Practicing non-killing, non-injuring, bodily and mental discipline, we must keep ourselves unspotted by the world. This does not, however, imply staying away from the world. It simply means to remain aloof from selfishness and greed and all the things that tie us to the material realm—this *rajasic* plane which is one of constant struggle.

Little by little, as our recognition of the spiritual increases, we discover a deep longing to attain to the higher plane and lesser things commence to drop away. The struggle then is no longer against the lower nature; no longer is the victory attained by battle as it is in the middle and lower realms. The whole conquest in this third world—the state if *sattva*—is made by keeping our eyes fixed on the Ideal. The conditions of outer life, the daily struggle, count for nothing when we are serving the spiritual Ideal; our whole life is focused on that one point. Then day by day our failures and successes make but passing impressions on us; even our own little human nature becomes of secondary interest. There is always that supreme Light and all values are measured against it. In the middle realm, whenever we pray or meditate we are concentrating on our own problems; we are trying to overcome some temptation or solve some difficulty. The whole thought is of ourselves, of trying to better ourselves. If we pray it is, "Give me something—give me light; give me strength." But when we have passed out of the middle realm our whole thought simply flows out in adoration to the Supreme.

We can help ourselves reach that state by constantly trying to think of something higher and thus gradually lift ourselves into it. It is a condition of balance where we are not continually moving up and down the scale—sometimes happy, sometimes miserable; sometimes doubting, sometimes full of faith. Once we have attained the higher realm, the Self is always there watching and we no longer identify ourselves with the lesser. We see it but it does not touch us. We remain as a witness.

Man in the lowest realm is scarcely active; he is dull, and content to go the round of his fleshly, selfish life. In the middle realm he is always in battle; he cannot look on; his consciousness is caught in the struggle. But in the third realm man is the witness, calm, serene, mighty. Even that is, however, not the end. One may have performed his life's duties; he may wish to live with the utmost simplicity in quiet surroundings, but his consciousness is still in the material. For even our highest thought is an individual point of matter. By the practice of purity in the state of *sattva*, serene, detached, selfless, man can reach the very limits of this world. But it is only when all his desires have gone or have been gathered up in that one intense desire for God when the hunger for the highest overtakes all other hungers, when the love for the Ideal transcends all other loves and he knows that there is no duty on earth so great as the search for the Supreme, then and then only does he transcend the three worlds of creation and see God face to face.

You may ask, "What then will become of our duties?" For the first time we shall do them well, because we shall go forth with the knowledge and power of a Buddha or a Christ, and all our tasks, great and small, will be perfectly done. If we enter a room everyone there will feel a blessing put upon him. If we speak even the simplest word a new life and courage will go with it to those who hear. Our living, our very being will uplift and purify and pacify every living thing. This must be the final duty of every man. We can linger as long as we wish in any of the three worlds; God is infinitely patient. He does not wish to see us suffer; He constantly calls to us, "Come up into the sunlight of your own highest being." This call is in our hearts at every moment; therefore, we are never contented.

We are meant to be eternal; we are meant to be infinite; we are meant to be ever-blissful. Until we are that we shall be given no rest, because the Soul within us is calling and it goes on calling until we are one with the Infinite—as Christ said, "One with the Father in Heaven", in conscious union with the Divine, knowing ourselves to be part and parcel of That which is the source of all worlds and which eternally transcends them.

MORALITY AND SPIRITUALITY
by Swami Saradananda

an there be any high philosophy or religion possible without a high standard of morals? The answer which the Vedanta gives to this question is always in the negative. No one can rise to the highest stage of spirituality without being perfectly and absolutely pure and high in point of morality. Examine the lives of the Vedic *Rishis* ("the Seers of thoughts") who attained to superconsciousness; or of Buddha, or Christ, or Sankara, or Chaitanya; were they pure or impure men? Has God ever manifested Himself through an impure channel? Never. These founders of the different religions have always been men pure in thought, word and deed; and what did they teach, every one of them? That morality must be the basis, the foundation, upon which spiritual life should stand; it must be the corner-stone of the spiritual building. Here the Vedic *Rishis* and all the Prophets of other religions are at one. The one great point of the teachings of the Vedanta, however, is that man's spiritual evolution does not stop with the evolution of a high code of ethics alone, but that there is another higher step to which he can reach, another link in this process of evolution and involution which completes the circle. And this is to be gained, not by denying, but by the fulfilling of all laws; not by throwing overboard all duties, but by the right performance of all duties; not by discarding society, but by being useful members of it; not by contracting the self, but by expanding it to its farthest limit; not by a man's thinking of himself as a cut and dried entity separate from the universe, but by feeling and realizing that he is one with this universe.

This universe according to Ramanuja, the great leader of the Qualified Monists in India, has been produced by the contraction of the knowledge of the soul, by the soul's forgetting that it is the storehouse of all knowledge and bliss and that it is one with the Infinite Ocean of Knowledge, which forms the background of the universe and is called God, the Absolute, *Brahman, Atman,* by so many different names. And liberation is to be attained by the expansion of the knowledge of the soul, when it will feel its union with the Divine and with the universe, which is nothing but a projection out of the Divine. Monism goes only a step further than the position of Ramanuja and teaches that perfect liberation is to be attained when the individual soul will not only feel this union and see the unity in the sum-total of all these differentiations, but will feel its identity with the Deity. This stage the Vedanta describes as the state of realization or the superconscious. The three states of the human mind,—the subconscious, the conscious, and the superconscious, are not three distinct minds, but the three different stages of one and the same mind. Modern science has discovered the process in the theory of evolution,—how the subconscious develops into the middle plane, the conscious existence, and the Vedanta is one with it as far as it goes; but it says further that this leaves the evolution (or as the Vedanta says, the involution) incomplete; the conscious will have to develop into the superconscious, and then alone will the process be complete. All our struggles, individual, social and human, are for that end, trying to gain that higher stage. There alone will man find the permanent basis of ethics, of religion, of everything. There, if an illiterate man enters, he will come out a sage, a prophet. The founders of the different religions, the religious giants whom the world has produced and will produce in the future, have been and will be men who have raised and will raise themselves to this higher stage. This is the stage which was described by Buddha as *Nirvana*; by Christ as being one with the Father; by the Mohammedan Sufis as *Analhak*, union with the truth; and in the famous aphorisms of the Vedanta as "Thou art that Infinite Ocean of Knowledge and Bliss," or "I am that Absolute *Brahman*."

The universe according to the Vedanta is one indivisible whole. It is by mistake that we think ourselves separate from the rest of the world. In the external world our bodies represent so many different points in the one vast ocean of matter, in which there is no break. Behind that lies expanded the one universal ocean of mind in which our minds but represent so many different whirlpools; and behind that even is the Soul, the Self, the *Atman*, the storehouse of all knowledge, power and bliss. So, though there is but one soul shining above, there are so many millions of reflections on the millions of whirlpools in the mental ocean; and these reflections are nothing

but so many individual egos. When a man raises himself to the superconscious, he sees the One Sun that
is shining above the mental ocean and he knows that
he is not a particular reflection but the Sun himself,
who has given rise to all the reflections in the ocean
of fine matter called the mind. And where lies the
basis of all ethics? In the fact that I am one with
and not separate from the universe; that in injuring
you I injure myself, in loving you I love myself; in the
fact that behind the manifold diversity there is a
unity, or, as the Vedantist says, behind these names
and forms there is that one eternal, unchangeable
ocean of Knowledge and Bliss which is our real nature. "This universe has been projected out of that
Ocean of Bliss Absolute." That Divinity is trying to
manifest itself through all these names and forms, and
the evolution of nature into higher and higher forms
is caused by this struggle of the Divinity within to
manifest itself better and better.

Every form or organism is a conduit through
which that Divinity is trying to manifest, and all that
we need to do is to remove the barriers which ob-
struct this flow of the Infinite within. With every act
of love and sympathy, every performance of duty,
every observance of morality, man is trying to go beyond himself by feeling himself one with the universe.
He is abnegating his lower self, and does not in this
self-abnegation lie the basis of all ethics? Examine all
the ethical codes which the world has ever produced
and you will find this one great fact taught,—to live
up to the higher Self by denying the lower. Consciously or unconsciously, every code of ethics is leading to that. They may not give you adequate reasons

why a man shall be moral and deny himself, but are we not thinking according to the laws of logic in every act of reasoning though we may not have read a single page of logic? The Vedanta supplies the reason why we shall be moral, why we shall do good to others, why we shall love all humanity as ourselves. Behind all these varied codes of ethics lurks that one great truth that we are one with the universe.

He who lives up to that one central truth has truly renounced himself. He who does not know this truth but tries to become a perfectly moral man, in thought, word and deed, he too is unconsciously living up to that truth. This word renunciation has got a very bad name nowadays. Yet every religion has enforced it often. It is the cornerstone upon which all religions, all ethics, have been built. Nay we are practising it every day of our lives, consciously or unconsciously. A man loves his wife, his children, his country, what is he doing all the time? Is he not renouncing himself? True renunciation, which every religion teaches, does not consist in isolating oneself from everything and every being, but in expanding oneself more and more widely, embracing the whole of the universe in oneself by love. For not in isolation or contraction but in expansion consists life and progress; this is the teaching of the Vedanta.

THEORY AND PRACTICE
by Sister Devamata

I n every department of nature we find the two sides, theory and practice, thought and word, will and deed. A life is strong just in proportion as the will takes shape in deed, as the theory is made a fact in practice. A life of mere theory is always a life of unhappiness. Nowhere is a man happy who is trying to make his word take the place of his deed, when he is pretending to be one thing and being another, when he is making a claim to something he is not. This is especially true in the realm of religion.

Yet, curiously enough, in religion alone theory stands accepted. Not long ago someone said that Christianity was an untried experiment. In the beginning a few people tried it, found it too difficult and gave it up, and the world has gone on with the theory of Christianity ever since.

As a matter of fact, a man is not religious until he begins to practice. Do you consider a man traveled who sits at home all his life and reads about other countries? Yet we consider a man religious if he goes to church every Sunday, hears about God, and knows nothing about Him. He hears about virtue and practices it very indifferently. He hears about illumination and realization and has not even a glimmering idea of what the words mean.

People go from place to place. They listen constantly to teaching. They have an idea that they are universal if they hear a Christian sermon in the morning and some New Thought teaching in the afternoon and another kind at night. They think that by running hither and thither they have a great interest in spiritual things; that the more things they can sympathize with and not understand, the broader they are. Their life is so full of theory that there is no room or time for practice. As a matter of fact, religion begins the day people stop running about, the day they stop talking, the moment they begin doing.

We cannot mix up methods in religion any more than we can mix up methods in music. Can we imagine anyone who wishes to learn to sing taking a lesson from one teacher on Monday, another teacher on Tuesday, and another teacher on Wednesday, and saying that this is done in order to have a true idea of music? That person will never learn to sing. We must take up one method and follow it until it is proved to be either good or bad. We must take up one systematic training, exactly as a child does in school. It is the only way we can advance.

Our knowledge of things is on a level with our experience of them. Reading, learning about religion, can never be a substitute for religion. Reading will never bring us to realization. We read our own limitation into every book.

The story is told of Sri Ramakrishna, that he went to his brother's college in Calcutta but stayed only a few weeks. He said one day while he was there, a priest—he was very learned—came home with some

bananas and a few pennies in his hand. Sri
Ramakrishna asked where he had got them, and the
man said he had earned them chanting. Then Sri
Ramakrishna said, "Is that all your learning brings
you?" He closed his book. "I want what will bring me
something loftier than that. When I have found out
God's thought, then I shall know whether man's
thoughts are true."

Religious reading is mere theory. The only practice is when we begin to read our own heart and our
own mind. That is the only book for the earnest man
who is seeking to know God. We must discover that
within ourselves which responds to that which is in
the book. Never can we read above our own understanding. A frog living in a well cannot imagine anything larger than his well. He is not peculiar. It is literally true of every living being. We can only inter-
pret a thought according to our own experience; truth
is the measure of our understanding. We think we
read books to enlarge our mind, and we merely con-
tract the books to the size of our mind. It is always so.

The only thing we can get out of a book is to
take what little we understand and begin to practice
it. What does the practice do? If we take the thing
we read today, practice it for a week, and then read
it again, we will find out. It is not enough merely to
think about what we have read. It must be practiced.

Yet we still must have the theory from day to day.
We must listen to it constantly. We must read it in
the scriptures, in the place where it is stated with realization; that is the difference. Ordinary literature is
all theory. Sacred literature, the scriptures alone, give
the virtue of practice and realization.

Many people today prefer to read books on science. Why? Because the man is telling something he has seen, experienced, practiced. That is the secret of the whole reaction against scholasticism, against theology, against all the old church teaching. "I have a theory and you have a theory. Now you come and hear my theory and see if you won't like it better." Each one has what he thinks is a more intelligent theory to take the place of your less intelligent one. But the scientist says: "I have cut this up and I know that it is so. I have watched this grow and I know that it is so." People want to get the absolute fact.

Now true scripture, if one knows how to read it, is just as scientific. As much of Christ as we get in the Bible, so much of the truth we have. When he says a thing, he knows it; he has seen it; just as the geologist has seen the structure of the earth.

So it is with the Vedic writings. The ancient *rishis* saw those things. They have taken the geologist's hammers, as it were, and broken up the structure of God's universe and discovered the cosmic secret. That is the reason why, if a man wants to read, he is told to go and read the scriptures—because he is reading of practice; he is not reading theories. So the man must go to the place where the scriptures are expounded and hear them, and then begin to practice them.

In Vedanta we are told there are three stages in the religious life. The first one is to hear the truth. The second one is to ponder upon it; and the third, which comes of itself, is the realization of it. We find exactly the same thing is true in science of any kind. One who has not studied, will not know. We do not need to know everything that Christ said, nor is it necessary to know the Bhagavad-Gita by heart, from beginning to end. But we do need to take one theory, one proposition, no matter what it is, and begin to ponder upon it; think it out; work it out as if it were a geometrical figure in our own mind, and see what we get out of it.

There is one more thing to learn in this religious practice: that is not to take all the propositions at once. When you hear that you must learn to read, you do not read the first, second, and third readers all at the same time. You begin quietly and read the first. So it is in religious practice.

Take it on the moral plane. Are you prone to anger? Let us take this as our proposition. What is the cause? Perhaps you have been trying to control anger all your life and still you have not been able to do it. Therefore your method must be wrong. Then you study; you ask yourself questions: Why should you care if you are insulted, or if your rights are impinged upon, or if a thing gives you pleasure or gives you pain? You may even make up a geometrical figure out of all this. By and by you become so interested in watching the problem develop that you almost forget to become angry. Begin to work on yourself at the point where your anger first rises. Go within yourself; deep down, and find that thing which gets angry; make that restless. Deal with your own ego. Find that thing within yourself that is above anger and desire— because desire is behind it—and devote all your spare time to working at that problem.

Do not work on anger today and discontent tomorrow and the love of riches the next day. No, work on the question of anger until you have solved it. It is a very curious thing that when you have solved one problem you have solved them all, because when you have found in yourself that thing which gets angry and that thing which nothing can touch, you have found that which will solve all your problems. Then your work is done. In no other way can you possibly have a stable religious life. So long as you are working only from theory, at any moment you can be confounded. If a man who has read a great deal about Paris but has never been there, makes a statement which is contradicted by someone who has lived in Paris, then he is discomfited, confounded.

It is the same with religion. That is why one who is not sure in his faith is open to doubt at any moment. He does not really know whether God exists. Doubt is at the bottom of all weakness, and doubt is the misery of a theoretical life. Our jealousy, our discontent, all spring from doubt. All of the evil passions spring from doubt. The Bhagavad-Gita says, "He who has doubt in his soul perishes." And doubt is always the misery of theory.

How can you be sure of a thing if you have not experienced it? In religious practice you must take each thing and prove it. You do not spend your time in making empty statements about something you have not proved to be true. When once you have the least bit of spiritual experience, nothing can shake you. You only smile when people tell you religion is not true.

I do not believe there are ten people in this city today who can stand up and actually say they believe in God. They think they do, but their whole life proves that they do not. If they heard that someone they loved more than anybody else in the world was in town, would they not go quickly to that person? Yet people stand up in church and in the pulpit, and say they love and believe in God, but they do not make the least effort to go and find Him. It is proof they do not believe in God, for what is God?

They say He is all-beauty, all-power, all-glory, all-life. Now if anyone actually believed that, would he rest one moment until he had found Him? When we really come to the awakening that God exists and that He is the thing that we say He is, we shall not rest night or day until we find Him. We will not say He is this or that, immanent or extra-cosmic. What do we care what He is? We want to go and see it for ourselves.

If I am looking for the source of the great beauty, and if you cannot tell me how to get to Him, that is all. Go about your business and I will look elsewhere. Swami Vivekananda was in this state when he was a boy of eighteen, and went hither and thither. There had risen in him a determination that if God was anywhere he would find Him. He went from one holy man to another and asked, "Do you believe in God and pray to Him? Have you seen Him? Then how can you know?"

In Calcutta he was looked upon as a skeptic because he would go to this place and that, where they were singing the praises of the Lord, and ask, "Why are you singing the praises of somebody you have never seen?" He came to Sri Ramakrishna and said to him, "Do you believe in God?" "Yes." "Have you seen Him?" "Yes." "Can you show Him to me?" "Yes." That was enough. From that moment he followed Sri Ramakrishna. Nothing ever turned him aside. Here was a man who had seen God, to whom God was reality.

But people say, "How can you see Him? You cannot. That is all nonsense."

Do you suppose that God, who has made Himself visible in all of His universe, in all of these myriad forms, in all this play of power and glory and wonder, cannot make Himself visible to you in just the form that you can best comprehend? Since he is omnipotent He has the power to come to you in any dress, to show Himself to you in any form. That was what happened in that wonderful chapter on transfiguration in the Gita. Arjuna said, "Show me Thy Lordly form. I have thought of Thee as a friend and teacher; now I desire to see Thee as Thou art." Krishna replied, "Thou canst not see Me with these eyes of thine. Do not try. It is no use. But, behold, I give thee the divine eye."

When any man longs for God, not in mere words, not by reading books about Him, not by going to a church or a temple to worship Him, but longs for Him enough to travel night and day to reach Him to make every activity of his life, every effort of his heart carry him towards God until his whole being is one quivering call for the divine, God never refuses to manifest Himself to that man. He will come whether the man is lettered or unlettered. Nothing matters. God will show Himself to that man as that man can comprehend Him; and having seen Him in that form, there will come into his mind and heart such realization, such understanding that he can comprehend God in all forms.

Give up all this intellectual seeking for God. Be earnest.   Never for a moment forget your purpose and longing for God. You need not have a scripture, you need not even have a theory, you need not have a name for God. You need have only your own soul and its earnest longing for Truth, then you will flourish and bear fruit. You will be a tree such as has been described in the Bible, upon which the birds came and lodged in its branches, and which brought freshness and life and nourishment to all the world.

That is all you need; just such earnestness, long-ing, and determination to embody in your life as much of truth as you know today, with a firm belief that out of that practice will come each day a larger and greater knowledge of the absolute Truth.

EDITORIAL—1914
by Paramananda

ri Ramakrishna tells the story of a man who, desiring to light the fire on his hearth at nightfall, took his lantern and went from door to door seeking a burning brand. Everywhere he asked in vain until at last he stopped before the threshold of a neighbor, who, wiser than the rest, looked at him wonderingly and said: "Foolish man, why are you begging a brand from me? Do you not see that in your own hand you have a light? Go home and kindle your fire with that." This is the message of Vedanta. It does not say: "You are in darkness, I will give you light." Or: "Your light is dim and dying; that which I bring you is strong and bright; blow out yours and take mine." On the contrary, it proclaims to every living being: "In your own heart burns the only light that can truly lighten you. By that alone can you kindle the fire of wisdom which will burn off all impurities and reveal the God within."

Every page of the Vedic Scriptures, in unparalleled variety of form and figure, reiterates this one supreme lesson. Truth can have no geographical or racial limitations. As a Galileo in Italy, a Euclid in Egypt, and Archimedes in Greece, or an Aryabhatta in India may discover a fundamental axiom in mathematics; so also the final vision of all things is possible to every mind that has the determination to strive for it, no matter what the creed or country. Ultimate attainment is not dependent on the acceptance of any personality or specific form of faith. Man must seek within and out of the depths of his own inner being evolve his creed; or as Christ has taught, "work out his own salvation". The various religions are so many methods to achieve this end; and since every constitution differs from every other, only that can be a universal religion or method which is capable of endless modification. Therefore it must be untrammeled by dogma or doctrine and commensurate with creation itself in scope. Such is the broad base upon which the great Himalayan Seers of the Vedas have reared their teaching. In it, as Max Muller declares, every phase of religion, from the lowest to the highest, finds a place. According to its comprehensive classification, all are only so many branches of a gigantic educational system, each fitted to the special needs of some soul and leading to the one common goal of supreme enlightenment or God-vision.

THOUGHTS ON VEDANTA
By Swami Saradananda

uch has been said regarding the su-
premacy of the system of philosophy and
religion revealed to the sages of India in
bygone prehistoric times and known to us as the
Vedanta. As affording a basis for reconciliation of all
the contradictory and hostile systems of thought, by
pointing to the one goal to which they have all been
tending; as supplying a proper and reasonable solution
of human life and its activities and of the good and
bad motives of conduct that move the individual as
well as the social and the national life in the world,
and that have been equally beneficial, through harmony or friction, for the uplifting of humanity; and
as upholding hopes of the highest enlightenment and
expression of power for sinner and saint alike, through
the mighty and irresistible processes of evolution, it
has for centuries been commanding the respect of sin-
cere and thoughtful men all over the world and will
continue to do so for ages to come. The great expo-
nents of Western pessimistic and optimistic thought,
Schopenhauer and Emerson, have both of them show-
ered praises on this system of Indian thought; and
have acknowledged their indebtedness for the spiritual
growth, the enlightenment, peace and solace that have
been brought by it and through it into their respec-

tive lives, moving in such opposite lines. Interested bodies may say what they please in their misdirected zeal for orthodoxy, but the glaring searchlights of the antiquarian, the philologist and students of the world's history, have proved again and again the fact that our world is one homogeneous whole and different nations and philosophies and religions, however independent and separate they may think themselves, are all related to one another for their respective growth and development, and are all indebted for some vital part or other to Indian civilization and Indian thought. System after system of philosophic and religious thought has arisen from this eternal fountainhead of wisdom and spirituality and has shed its blessings on the many, voicing the one message of concord and agreement. The claims of the spirit are recognized. "Man is not really what he seems to be. Infinite possibilities lie within him, as well as the power and the resources to bring them out. Deep in the heart of the infinite love and knowledge is his eternal abode, and never has he really lost the effulgent glory of his own absolute nature . . ."

Out from the heart of the Indian Scriptures flowed the religion of the Zend, which, arranged and expressed with added power by Zarathustra, gave such a stimulus to Christianity, by supplying the latter with many of its cardinal principles of sin, atonement and devotion through love. Out of it again "in the long-drawn aisles of time" came forth Buddhism, a beautiful child full of sympathy and love and service to all, that sent its messages of peace and love even to Asia Minor, where a few hundreds of years after the mighty "Man of sorrows" repeated them in almost the same words, while teaching in the mountains of the holy land. Testimonies are not wanting in this direction and innumerable instances can be brought forward from the pages of history. But it is sufficient for our purpose here to see the power and vitality which the religious thought of India possessed of old, and the stimulus it afforded to the many great religious movements of the world. Has it died out at the present day? Has it become "a bewildering festering pool of ignorance and superstition," as some of our contemporaries in and outside our country have been advised to call it, forgetting in their hasty and one-sided zeal the debt of gratitude and fellowship which they owe to Indian spiritual thought? Are there no mainsprings of life and conduct for guiding and regulating the individual society and nation, to be found in the system of Vedanta? Our little paper is to discuss this vital question touching the Indian religious life; and to throw some hints and suggestions to help bring in the light that has been dawning on the horizon of India. Infinite possibilities lie imbedded in the teachings of the sages of old; and the more we turn towards them with uplifted gaze and consider them in their practical bearings, for the guidance and regulation of the conduct of the individual, the clearer becomes the vision of the future glory of the country. For societies and nations are but aggregates of different individual units; and a system of religion and philosophy which has the power of directing the conduct of those units to higher and higher ends, cannot but help to ennoble and uplift the social and national standard.

In studying the religious history of the world, the one fact that becomes most obvious to the mind of the student is that all the great religions have begun with pessimism and painted the life of man on this side of the grave in dark colors. It is natural and easy for a man to take to this dark view of life, considering the thousand and one difficulties that beset his path in his travel through this vale of sorrow and tears, the thousand and one hopes that are crushed to pieces even from his childhood, and the many disappointments that crowd on his heels in this "two days existence". The unrequited love, the faithlessness of many, the hard struggle and competition, the wicked in power, misery, disease and pain—all serve their quota in making him take refuge in this cynical view of human existence. "Turn your eyes away from this life and its miseries and strive to gain that life beyond the grave, where happiness reigns supreme and all inequalities of human conditions are smoothed down by a divine and loving hand"—thus say the Scriptures of the nations. Call after call goes out to bring man to this higher existence; and the life here and that hereafter are viewed as two entirely different things, so that man must give up one in order to find the other. Examine the ethics of Buddhism, of Christianity, of the Koran and the Avesta in the light of the lives and the teachings of their founders and of the first upholders of the respective faiths, and you will find this common strain of pessimism running through them all.

Pessimism, having thus given an aberrant vision of the world and human existence, brought forth the doctrine of suppression of the powers that lead man towards this life and its ill-afforded happiness. "Kill the flesh by all means"; "Death to the old man, who casts a longing look at this side of existence"; "The body is a festering mass of corruption, turn thou away from it"—all these ideas became the motive power of religion. Different means of torturing the body by starvation and decimation came to light and were regarded as so many means of salvation. Alas for human ignorance! Little did man dream that though the body should not be allowed to master the mind and the Self, yet it was the only instrument in his hands to attain to higher enlightenment and should therefore be taken care of to a certain extent.

Religion sounded a different note altogether in the hands of Sri Krishna and the Yogis, who boldly asserted that not killing the flesh, but controlling and keeping it within proper bounds, will help man to realize the highest end; and that such was the meaning of the Vedas. "Control the activities of the senses from going into lower channels; waste not your energies by unnecessary privations, but regulate your food, your sleep and every other affair of life and be pure in thought, word and deed"—thus say the Gita and Patanjali in loud tone. But the death-knell of pessimism was sounded by the discovery of progress through evolution by Kapila. It was weak at first and a mere theory; but it slowly but surely gathered strength and gained ground, till modern science came to its help and support with all the panoply of objective methods of proof. The wonderful discovery that force and matter are both indestructible; that both of these on examination afford infinite suggestions of being the modifications of one common substance; that the sum total of energy in the universe is always the same, whether it remains in the kinetic or potential

form; that different forces are correlated and inter-
changeable; and that nature is uniform throughout her
work and always working with the same materials in
the same way on the different planes of existence, the
physical, the mental and the spiritual—all this has
helped us understand and express that old doctrine of
Kapila better and with added power, and has given a
new stimulus to religion all over the world.

Many a religion has had to change its tone, in
adapting itself to this new light of science and reason;
and many are lagging behind with faltering steps, unable to adapt and assimilate these innovations. Had
we ever to do that? Had we ever to give up the one
cardinal principle of the religion of the Vedas, the
dharma that has been founded on the rock of evolution? Thanks to the sages of old, though a little mor-
tar here or cement there may have fallen down under the bombardment of science, the frame work of
the hallowed structure proved strong enough to bear
the brunt of the fight; and it required but little effort and concession to make peace and cooperate with
the enemy. True science is never an enemy to true
religion; its wars in all ages have been with ignorance
and superstition and bigotry.

Is there no future possibility for that religion,
which has been teaching the homogeneity of the universe from the earliest dawn of history, and the infinite progress of each unit in it through evolution,
functioning on all planes of being and placing the
motive power of it (that evolution) in the Self within?
Can there be no vitality in the Scripture that teaches
that the soul is beyond all creed, color and sex and
that the highest enlightenment may be gained by all

alike? Turn to the pages of the Vedas and you will find that revelation and vision transcending the senses have come both to men and women alike. Be strong, say the Vedas; depend upon your innate strength; let neither happiness nor misery turn you away from the pursuit of the highest ideal; take easily the changes that life brings every moment, recognizing that you have brought them upon yourself, and remember that you have the power of changing them again; above all, move in cooperation with nature, within and without, knowing that the God within you is ever giving powerful support. Thus alone can man transmute all his energies to the highest ends and develop his present limited consciousness to the unlimited supraconscious existence.

THOUGHT RELICS
1912—1940
by Paramananda

Today we are facing a new phase in our human evolution. It is no longer a matter of what religion we have...fundamentally there is no difference between them.

Spiritual life is not following some creed, it is evolving the Spirit within us, and that does not come accidently.

We have separated ourselves from the great Ocean of Being and this separation is the cause of all our ailments, chronic and acute...A man must be connected with That which is abiding—his whole life depends upon it.

Dwell upon immortal thoughts. This is the secret of self-preservation, of the renewing of oneself. Keep your heart free, free and pure! Let it circulate pure thoughts.

T he Kingdom of Heaven is something which happens within us.

℘

M any times we go into a temple, or a great house of worship, and find no point of contact there, and the next moment, perhaps, without any occasion, with no setting and nothing whatsoever in the way of outer glamour, we make a living connection with our innermost being. How do we account for these things? Wherein lies the secret? It lies in our faith, our feeling.

℘

O ften I have spoken of the significance of feeling a Divine Presence in our life, a Presence so constant, permeating and pervading that as long as we are aware of it, nothing can molest or thwart our purpose. That is the dawning of our spiritual consciousness.

℘

E veryone must evolve his spiritual consciousness...When it comes to the practical working out of our spiritual destiny, every individual must do that for himself or herself, because there is no power which stands between us and God from Whom we have ascended. As soon as we become aware of this fact, all feelings of anxiety, all that is petty and small vanish, and we begin to partake of a larger life.

If we carry the joy of God in our hearts,
others will feel it—for the joy of God is also infectious.

G.

Without His will not a blade of grass moves...
The average person may ask, but why should a blade of
grass have anything to do with the Divine Will? There is
nothing that happens outside of that Will. Pleasant or
unpleasant are included within it... He is working through
us and with us in the fulfillment of his infinite Purpose.

G.

We have only to hold one thought—that we
are being used by the Great Power to work out great
Spiritual problems.

G.

If we can abandon our fears and anxieties,
the Power within will not fail us... It may burn dim,
but that which burns dimly, by our effort can be made to
burn brightly.

G.

We are placed here by a Divine Hand and are
fulfilling a Divine Purpose.

H ere is the secret of happiness: Forget yourself and think of others... When you feel dull, heavy and
depressed, it is because you are thinking of yourself...
Love, serve and forget yourself.

G॰

W e are part of the world—each one of us—
and when our hearts are filled with joy, we make this
world more joyous.

G॰

O Man, pervade the whole world with the
consciousness of God. He is everything. That which you
see, whatever you perceive, all that exists, know that to
be God's form.

THREE POEMS
by Paramananda

Merit? Merit? Brother, who told thee I had
    merit?
Merit have I none, nor ever did I have.
What merit hath the straw?
The weaver shapes a basket with it.
If the basket be fair it is not the merit of
    the straw;
It is his skill who maketh it.
I am that straw which once lay at the great
    Weaver's feet.
But He, the Compassionate, took it in His
    hand and fashioned it.
Now I cherish this basket of His fashioning
To gather His blessing.

I am the Spirit of eternal
    youth.
I am form in infinite space.
I am unchanging beauty.
I am undying life.
Endless time am I.
I am order in chaos.
I am lull in the storm.
I am fury of the wind.
I am calm of the deep.
I am flash of the lightning.
I am dark of the wild.
I am crash of the thunder.
I am stillness of the night.
Perfume of the flowers am I.
Majesty of the mountains am I.
The quiet solitude of thy soul is my
    home
The peace of thy heart is my rest.

G.

When Thou art near, I feel
    strong and my heart
    sings a happy song.
When I lose Thee, all my
    strength fails me and darkness
    enshrouds my heart.
Lamp of my life,
Joy of my soul,
Vigor of my spirit art Thou!

SCRIPTURES

I am the origin of all, everything evolves from Me. Knowing this, the wise worship Me with loving ecstasy.

The Bhagavad-Gita 10:8

ॐ

I am the sage Kapila among the perfected one.

The Bhagavad-Gita 10:26

ॐ

The earth is the Lord's, and the fullness thereof; the world, and they that dwell therein.

Psm. 24:1

For by Him were all things created, that are in heaven, and that are in earth, visible and invisible . . . all things were created by Him and for Him.

Col. 1:16

Then Paul stood in the midst of Mars' hill, and said, Ye men of Athens, I perceive that in all things ye are too superstitious. For as I passed by and beheld your devotions, I found an altar with this inscription, TO THE UNKNOWN GOD. Whom therefore ye ignorantly worship, Him declare I unto you. God that made the world and all things therein, seeing that He is Lord of heaven and earth, dwelleth not in temples made with hands; neither is worshipped with men's hands, as though He needed anything, seeing He giveth to all life, and breath, and all things; and hath made of one blood all nations of men for to dwell on all the face of the earth, and hath determined the times before appointed, and the bounds of their habitation; that they should seek the Lord, if haply they might feel after Him and find Him, though He be not far from every one of us: For in Him we live and move and have our being.

Acts 17:22-28

INFINITE IN MAN
By *Swami Paramananda*

This subject may seem a very large order to one who is overwhelmed with his finite nature. Even the most intelligent among us recognize the limitations of the body, mind and brain. How, then, can we assume that the man before us, human and failing, can ever hope to claim to be related to the Infinite? Yet, for him to find his relationship—not in a theoretical way, but directly with the Supreme should be the great goal of his life, his most profound study. And this means that when he goes through his round of physical duties, and even when he is confronted with difficulties, he will seek to remind himself that he is part of that indivisible Whole.

Nowhere was this theme discussed, studied and contemplated as it was in India. The Hindus wanted to get away from the noise, turmoil and turbulence of the world, from those things which cause affliction, yet do not allow us to think of the higher and deeper things of life; so they entered into the depths of silence. That was the origin of the "Forest Books," as they called them,—the forest books of wisdom, and I am going to venture to give you some lessons from these great Scriptures of the Indo-Aryans.

Enter into thy closet—Christ said—shut the doors,

and then pray silently. We find this exemplified in the life and aspiration of those ancient people. They sought Truth for no other reason than for the sake of Truth Itself, recognizing It as the greatest factor in human existence, without which man's life is very much impoverished, so they made it their first and foremost thought, seeking with all the ardour of their soul to be related with It, transcending and transcending their finite nature until it altogether melted away before the glory of the Infinite, just as ice melts before the sun. Whenever these Indo-Aryan sages spoke to their disciples in regard to the grandeur of the soul, they were at the same time tremendously puzzled as to how they could convey the significance of it to a person who was seeing and perceiving things only with the senses.

Thus we find this conversation between a youth and one of these teachers to whom he had come for instruction: "Sire," said the youth, "teach me about this Infinite. You say that It is vast and unbounded. Tell me something more definite that I may comprehend: Where is It? How can I find It? Is It within the body? If so then why am I not able to know It?" The abstract Truth has always to be conveyed to the minds of people by concrete forms; that was the origin of parables. Christ's teaching is filled with them. Therefore the teacher said: "My boy, I shall try to give you a living illustration. Do you see that *nigrodha* tree standing there? Go and fetch me one of the fruit lying beneath it." The boy did as he was told and the master said: "Break it." "Sire, it is broken." "What do you find within?" "A large seed, Sire." "Break that and tell me what there is inside." And so the boy went on taking off layer after layer till he came to the invisible center. "What do you find at the heart of the seed?" enquired the teacher. "I find nothing, Sire," the boy replied. "Yet there," the sage explained, "where you see nothing, lies the real germ out of which this great tree has come into existence."

But the boy was not satisfied. This also seemed to him a riddle, that a big tree could spring out of what seemed like nothing; yet he was interested, so he said: "Master, tell me more about that life within." "Very well," said the sage, "bring to me a glass of water and a lump of salt, place the salt in the water and come back in the morning." This the disciple did and returned the next day full of keen desire to know how a glass of water and a lump of salt could illustrate the Vast and Unlimited. As soon as he came, the teacher said: "Where is the lump of salt that you put in the water?" The boy looked but naturally could not find it. "Taste the water from the surface; what is its flavor?" "It is full of salt, Sire." Taste it from the middle." "It is still full of salt." "Taste it from the bottom." "That also is full of salt." "My son," the sage replied, "as this water is filled with salt which you taste yet cannot see, similarly this whole universe is pervaded and permeated by That which is invisible to the eyes." This was convincing. He sensed the salt, he tasted it, yet it was not perceptible to his mortal sight. Thus he was shown the connection between the finite and the Infinite.

It is only when our subtle intellect is quickened with intensity of feeling that we begin to know about that great Absolute. We cannot, however, advance in that knowledge so long as we allow our mind to remain buried in material desires, in selfishness, greed, avarice, jealousy, hatred, narrowness, or any of those elements which spring from the flesh. By continuing to cling to them, we keep on depriving ourselves of that which sustains us. The Bible tells us, all Bibles tell us—I cannot make any exception—that we must become like unto our Origin,—be perfect as our Father which is in Heaven, or, as the Indo-Aryan sages reminded their children: Know that there is an infinite, unbounded, invincible, indivisible, unalterable *Purusha* (Being), and that Being exists in thee. How does it exist? "As from the blazing fire burst thousands of sparks like unto the fire, so also, gentle youth, do the various beings spring forth from the Imperishable and return thither again."

Let us pause for a moment. We do not think in these terms. If some wise man, or a Christ comes and tells us that we are possessors of Infinitude, we feel puzzled. If we are cynical we may say, "This man is mad." Many people thought that Christ was. Whenever such a voice speaks, we are apt to think that it sounds the note of extremes, not recognizing that it is we who have lost a sense of balance and proportion. "Know thyself; thou art That." A statement like this is dazzling to us and we feel that we must go slowly. We begin to analyze: If we have any connection whatsoever with that vast unbounded Life—immortal and indestructible—why is it we are afflicted, why are we conscious of limitation? The trouble is, we are thinking of one aspect of our being, they are speaking of another, and that other is within us. Just as the sword is in the sheath, and the germ of life in the fruit, so in man there is this inner Spirit con-

cealed by a shell, an outer covering. The thing is how
to find it and not be prejudiced by the exterior. We
are prejudiced. If I should ask you, "Who are you?"
and put down your answer side by side with the reflections of the great teachers, I should find at once
that it was influenced by your mental concept of the
physical. We are thinking thoughts and making admis-
sions constantly about ourselves which are neither becoming, nor representative of our true nature. When
a man forms a selfish concept of his own entity, he
feels that he must think of himself in selfish terms,
must assert his rights and be aggressive in order to
protect his interests; but by this he is really lowering
himself. Of course we have to speak of these things
with a certain reservation. The average person does
not think in this way. He might hold that I was
teaching false philosophy.

Spiritual grandeur is not a question of pretending.
The point is we must know our own value. From
what point of view are we speaking? From what point
of view are we acting, and from what point of view
are we influencing the world consciousness? That is
the question, and it is the thing which determines our
destiny. We are thinking of the finite in connection
with ourselves and that makes us feel suffocated. We
center ourselves upon some small interest; we dwell on
those things which are connected only with our own
personal happiness, with the life of the flesh, till by
reason of our increasing limitations, we impose upon
ourselves every reason for suffering. I do not know
whether I convey the idea to you; but this narrowing
down of consciousness is the real cause of our afflictions. No matter how much we have in the way of

material wealth, life becomes a weight upon us when we take it in this way. "What shall it profit a man if he gains the whole world . . . ?" Christ gave this warning for all humanity, not for a little portion of it. "And what can a man give in exchange for his soul?" That is the great challenge, and it is where we find the clash between the finite and the Infinite.

Can we ever be satisfied—being reminded constantly that we are bound? If we go out, we may catch cold; if we do this or that we may get hurt; if we have an impulse to help some one, we must not do so because we shall have less for ourselves. Such thoughts we consider wise for self-preservation, but they spring from a lower source, and until we can break these fetters, we cannot come in touch with a Higher. This is done through understanding—understanding our own worth, as I have said, not in the terms of materiality,—how much money we have put away in the bank, or what a name we have acquired in the struggle of physical life,—not that; but our true worth, our relationship to God the Absolute, the Infinite. It is consciousness of this, that gives man the power to govern his own destiny, to conduct himself through all the various passages of life, and to aid others. He establishes a standard for living.

You may say, "My mind does not go so far; I am concerned only with what will give me a good, healthy body and a certain amount of peace and happiness." But a certain amount is not going to satisfy us. There is within us a Divine Spark—we are part of that great Effulgence; It is our heritage. Until we know it consciously, however, and are able to put it into practice, we have not yet unfolded our entire nature; we have not wholly developed. You may imagine that such consciousness will make us aggressive. If man suddenly becomes aware that he carries within him the Infinite Spirit, will he not become domineering and seek to rule over others? It works in the opposite way. Knowledge—wisdom—makes a person very mellow. Harmfulness in the world does not come from people who are great. Small people may misunderstand us, they may harm us, we may fear to approach them, but the men of genius, the men of perception, those who have contacted in some way or another this inner Spirit, are very humble. It is not a calculated humility,—that they give a little smile here and a little pretense there in order to gain popularity; it is something that springs from within, spontaneously, and it is that spontaneous something which we must gain before we can find our true Self-expression.

We want to be shown what we call miracles and mysteries. We are always seeking for signs, as if any sign could convince us. What more do we require than that we have life, that we have intelligence, are endowed with all these fine faculties? The point is, are we making the best of them? Do we know the worth of love and have we learned to be governed by the instinct of love and to banish all hatred from our hearts? Realization of the Infinite is not a dogma or a doctrine written down in a book; it is a consciousness we have to unfold. Man has gradually to break through his finite, limited barriers, and at the outset it seems like a very difficult task. He may feel that it is too much for him; but nobody else is going to do it for him. We do not depend on others to eat, drink or sleep for us, so why should we in this? One of the questions that often comes up is that if Christ realized that Infinite, if He brought salvation to the world, why was it not accomplished for all time? If the great saviours, saints and sages bring wisdom why is it not sufficing for us? It would be if we only would walk on the same path, if we would make our hearts like theirs. We cannot, however, turn our eyes in another direction and expect to find their vision.

"That Effulgent Being, He is within man and He is without man." It is not that we should condemn the flesh. I do not want you to go away with the idea that in speaking of the Infinite, or the vast subtle life within, that I would have you ignore the physical life. It would be going to another extreme. "He exists both within and without. He is everywhere." When you have the perception to know that Great Being, innate, operating this whole mechanism of life—body, mind, senses, brain, heart,—every pulsation of our being, then you no longer go into the world of action unarmed and unprepared. You will have found a definite point of contact with the source and this is what makes all the difference in our actions and in our dealings. Your own thought, your own understanding spirit can bring you untold successes and protection. When you become a conscious instrument of that great Infinite, there is nothing that can hinder you. Through you this Light will radiate Itself into the world of life, into the hearts of men.

You may challenge this. You may say, "I have tried but it does not work out. The times I have held the kindest thoughts and the most loving feelings, people have proved untrustworthy, have deceived me." This is to accept failure. It means that you have not yet the amount of conviction that you need. We should not put this matter on the basis of bargaining and bartering, practising an ideal with the one idea to see how much we can gain. The question is, from what point of view are we going to work? Shall we fasten our heart and mind, our interest and our aim on the flesh? Shall we depend on our muscle or on what operates our muscle? On the mental capacity we have, or on that which operates the mind? We must go deeper and deeper. Today we have formed the habit of living very much on the surface, and see the result of this surface living! People smile when they don't feel like smiling, they say things they do not mean at all; it is causing a tremendous amount of misunderstanding, not only in the world at large, but in families. And what does it show? Emptiness—lack of faith. It means that we are not really thinking, that we are acting in a mechanical way as if we were machines; therefore we must cultivate a more profound attitude toward life, because the whole strength of man lies embedded within.

It is not that a few people who are predestined, come into the world with this power and because of it, rise to a great height; we all have it. There is not a soul who does not possess this inner strength. Has not the great Upanishad declared that we are like a spark from the Divine Fire? Nothing can extinguish that blazing flame. Emerson uses the same expression. He was a great student of the Eastern Scriptures. He tells us that every man possesses within himself the Divine Spark. Unfortunately we have forgotten it. We do not know that we have that Spark within us; we think our house is absolutely in the dark and that we must borrow our light from others. There is a story of a man who actually did this. Coming home at night-fall, he found his fire had gone out. There was, how-ever, a very dim lamp burning in his room, so he took this to light his steps and went forth to beg a fire brand from his neighbors. At first they all re-fused—some people have that habit; but finally one looked out at him and exclaimed: "Foolish man! Why are you going begging from door to door when in your own hand there is a light. You think that it is dim and insufficient, but I tell you that small flame has enough power to set this whole village ablaze. Go home and light your own fire." So he did, and no longer was he dwelling in the dark, no longer was he cold and suffering.

This is a hint that we can all take. We go from place to place, carrying a heavy heart, a mournful spirit, a despondent attitude, thinking that others are going to help us, that we shall be given a magic word which will make us prosperous and forever free. The only thing that the wise give us, however, is to show us what we truly have and are. Our little light may seem inadequate, but if we add fuel to it, it will blaze forth and all our darkness and sadness will vanish, as night vanishes before the light of the day.

"When He is seen who is both high and low, the fetters of the heart are broken, all doubts are cut asun-der, and all *Karma* is destroyed." We have formed the habit of worshipping God only in churches or sanc-tuaries, but the man of wisdom finds Him everywhere. We speak of Him as Almighty and Omnipotent, but we do not put this idea into practice. We should try to see godliness and glory and all fine things even there where it is not so obvious, even in those who do not seem to manifest these attributes. "When we see Him in everything, all doubts are cut asunder and all bondage is destroyed." We do not have to struggle against these limitations; they fall automatically. This vision, this glimpse of Truth, this spiritual effulgence does away with all that is detrimental; through it we feel remade and requickened.

"That stainless indivisible *Brahman*, pure Light of all lights; dwells in the innermost golden sheath—the core of the heart." "Indivisible," that, I think, is one of the most interesting expressions of the Upanishads, yet how little we feel its significance. We even try to partition off the sky line, we are so concerned in asserting our rights, in defining what belongs to us. Therefore it is good for us to think in the terms of the Infinite in order that we may not be merged in limited, worthless, selfish thoughts; when we follow the path of aggressiveness, we meet with reaction and experience a sense of failure. When, however, we base our hopes on these higher ideals, this can never happen, because then we shall be connected all the time with that which can never fail.

"He dwells in the innermost recess of our being." Thus the knowers of Truth find Him within—within—in the depth of our real being. "The sun does not shine there, nor the moon, nor the stars, nor do these lightnings shine there, much less this fire. When He shines, everything shines after Him; by His light all is lighted." Thus the Upanishads tell man that even the sun and moon cannot reveal That. All this glamour and glory of material life, they are nothing; it is because He shines that all these things shine after Him.

What a wonderful lesson for us to learn! No matter how glorious we may become, or how much power may be bestowed upon us, let us never forget that all our strength and our blessings are dependent on that One. Even the sun draws its light from Him; and for us, to feel that we are a part of that Infinitude, to rely on It, to fasten our heart upon It, is the highest wisdom, the only way of salvation, the banishing of darkness from this world of misery.

DIVINE INSPIRATION
By Swami Paramananda

ivine inspiration comes quietly, so quietly that the individual is scarcely aware of its presence. It comes without any ostentation, yet the benediction it brings is unspeakably rich. Do not think even for a moment that it is only poets, artists, musicians and spiritual teachers who need inspiration and that the average man has nothing to do with it. In the entire humanity there is not one who can make his life a true contribution either to himself or to his fellow-beings without proper inspiration. When we lack it, life falls upon us as a heavy load. There are many in this world of ours who work, who fulfill their duties, but they feel the weight of them. They do them with a sense of drudgery; but we can perform our daily tasks with a very different feeling,—with love, with inspiration. We cannot undertake anything with love, exuberance and selfless devotion without its unfolding for us. We learn from that task every step of the way. We can never escape from the dead weight of life until we have this awakening.

Inspiration! It is a divine guidance; it is the greatest heritage of man. It fills all our drudgery full of love, beauty and upliftment. Unfortunately we often regard spiritual themes as something apart from our everyday life. In our daily activities we may not find the same possibilities for inspiration as we find in the lives of the master-spirits of the world. But why are they master-spirits? How have they become so great? Is their destiny specially mapped out for them; or have they made it possible for the great divine Power to flow through them? You know how it is if you neglect a mirror for days, weeks or perhaps months. Although the mirror still has the quality of reflecting, it does not reflect clearly and often even it distorts. Likewise when the surface of water is calm, clear and not agitated by wind, we see the clear reflection of our own image, or of trees, clouds, birds, or whatever comes near it. Are these not good illustrations of the human mind and heart? We long to accomplish great things in life; but in our haste and ambition, we altogether overlook the fact that unless our mind is serene, our heart fit for reflecting the Divine, we shut ourselves off from higher inspiration. Although we may work with our hands and our feet, if our mind is overactive and feverish with anxiety, nothing is accomplished. Often we bring about just the opposite result to that which we have set our hearts upon.

These things do not happen by accident. It is not that a man achieves success through chance. He does not find poetry pouring out of his soul by chance, he does not become beatified through chance. It is all, directly or indirectly, the sum total of what we are. We can make ourselves so susceptible to higher influences that no matter what comes before us we draw inspiration from it, as we see in the soul of a poet or mystic. A poet comes in contact with a tree or a rock, a river, a brook, a bird or a beast and it speaks to him. Everything speaks to him. Because he has a living soul, all Nature becomes living. But the man who is unconscious of this living soul within and whose thoughts and aspirations are not in harmony with that living soul, blocks the way to its expression. There is a great difference between one individual and another. It does not necessarily follow that when we are full of keen calculation, when we are very shrewd, that we are going to have inspiration. On the contrary, we sometimes hinder its manifestation through our calculation. When there is too much self-assertion, especially if the selfish aspect of our life is dominant, then that pure light cannot shine through us.

We individuals have a great deal to do with our life's unfoldment, with its success or failure. One who consciously or perhaps unconsciously, holds unkind, uncharitable thoughts, do you suppose his prayers will make him holy? Or that just because he professes an exalted creed he is going to gain true inspiration? No, a man may go on living quietly, humbly, without ostentation, without recognition; but if his heart is pure, if his soul is cleansed of all its selfish aspect, he will kindle the divine spark within him.

This brings a strange dilemma to our mind. If every man possesses the divine spark within, if every man has descended from that universal, cosmic Spirit, what difference can it make whether he knows it or not? There is a great difference between consciously possessing that great spiritual force and being unaware of it. No one can rob us of our immortality, no one can deprive us of our divine heritage; and yet we are deprived of it. A man may have inherited a fortune, yet if he is not aware of it or has no conscious control over it, it will do him no good. He will suffer just as though he did not possess it; he will worry and fret and sometimes even go through the agony of poverty. Same way is it with our life. We may have read in the Bible or in some Holy code that we are all descendants of one great Spirit, one infinite Being; but it avails us nothing unless we know it for ourselves; and without inspiration who can know about divine things? Going to church or professing a creed does not make us religious, not even though we are willing to fight for our creed, as many fanatics do in this world. Without inspiration every step of our way is fraught with danger. Our working life becomes very arduous. In our office, for instance, work hangs heavy over us; we feel the burden of it; we carry it like a great cross. Sometimes we curse our destiny, curse humanity and make life hideous. But one who knows how to carry that cross, glorifies it, just as we see in the example of Christ and in the example of all great saints, mystics and men of genius.

Often we come across people who are forever finding fault. They find fault with themselves, with their friends, with every one. Because their experience in this world has been full of evil, they trust no one. Full of suspicion, full of doubt, failure falls upon them at every step. In spite of all the religion they profess, they have no faith and their life becomes a mockery. Then again we come in contact with one who beautifies all things; whatever he touches breathes life and seems to give forth fragrance. This is not through chance. We all have the power to make ourselves channels for the divine Light, and also we can block the light in such measure that not only do we live in agony and despondency ourselves, but we throw that weight upon others. Some people make us feel that the only way out of life's unhappiness is through suicide. Others again fill us with enthusiasm, inspire us. Even in the midst of despair they give us the feeling that we can overcome all obstacles. Moments come when we have great difficulties; life presents a gruesome aspect; everything seems to go wrong and we face discouragement and failure. Should we settle down and accept defeat as a final thing?

There are two ways of looking at life. Some look at it as a material creation. They recognize its changing aspects and take only the facts which come through sense-evidence. When there is a stormy day with hours that are dark and threatening, they feel that the sun is never going to shine again. People of this nature magnify their troubles by brooding over them. But there are those who, no matter what troubles confront them, pierce through the veil of darkness and find their way beyond the clouds. Such is the nature of inspiration. It is like a divine spark. It is not something which comes to us with noise. That is why many of us miss it entirely. We are used to noise, used to hearing only that which is given with loud clamour. But there are things given subtly, which we do not perceive. That is why the individual should cultivate his finer perception, his subtler sense of hearing and sight. We can so train our mind and heart that we can hear the voice of the Unseen and are able to contact that which our physical senses cannot discern.

In one of the great Hindu classics there is an illustration of the coming of inspiration. One day as the sage and immortal poet Valmiki was going with his disciple to bathe in the river, he saw two birds playing together. He was rejoicing at their happiness when suddenly a hunter shot the male bird, causing the female bird to cry out in agony of soul. This shot not only pierced the heart of the little bird, it went to the heart of the sage, so that he broke forth in unaccustomed utterance: "O thou cruel hunter, success will never be thine, for thou hast caused the destruction of an inno-cent, love-intoxicated bird." Astounded at the beauty, the music and the power of his words, he turned to his disciple and asked, "What is this, my son? Have you ever before heard me speak in such lines?" "No Sire," replied the disciple. Again another Sanskrit verse came flowing through him, without any conscious seeking on his part for grandeur of language, rhythm or beauty. Then a voice told him the Spirit of the universe had bestowed upon him the gift of inspiration and he was appointed to write the life of great Rama, the ideal of manhood; and this book would not live just for a time and then be forgotten. "As long as the mountains shall exist," declared the voice, "as long as sun and moon shall shine and the rivers flow upon the earth, so long will people derive inspiration from thy gift"; and it was true. Indian history has proved it. In India children are brought up under the inspiration of the sage Valmiki. It was like a clarified stream flowing through him.

There is a great difference between what we do through force of circumstance and that which comes spontaneously, flowing from within. We all know this. We may not always be able to do everything spontane-ously, but why should we kill our spontaneity? That is one of the greatest tragedies of our modern life. We are always trying to crush down what is innate, what is pure, what is lovely, what is subtle; and we are forever running after that which is full of noise, glamour and ostentation. In this way we are deprived of the more beautiful aspect of our life. What we need is balance. It is not that we should all become visionary and sit with folded hands, waiting until we have inspiration. It does not come to us that way, but only as we make ourselves harmonious through our thought, our aspiration and our actions.

It is the divine right of every one of us to tune ourselves in such a way that we can draw from the divine Source. Are we not all children of the One? If we are not conscious of that, it makes no difference what religion we profess. It may have a big sounding name. We may be able to quote from the Bible, from the sacred classics, from all the loftiest sentiments of the world, but are we those things? Have we united ourselves with those feelings? Are we able to express them through our actions or words and our silent thoughts? If at present we are unable to do this, it does not mean that we are incapable of it. We must always make a start, no matter where we stand, and we must not start with a negative feeling. There is a very great difference in this respect between the Indo-Aryan message and the Semitic teachings. This difference rests in the emphasis laid upon the two aspects of life. The Indian sages tried to inspire their followers not so much by emphasizing the existence of sin and iniquity, but rather by bringing out that which is the opposite of sin. "Hear, ye children of immortal bliss!" There is something very majestic in that call.

It does not require any great genius to find fault with others; we can all of us do that. We can convince them that they are worthless, immersed in sin and sorrow. But this does not save a soul. When a man becomes conscious of his worthlessness, he sinks deeper and deeper; but when he becomes conscious that he has a saving grace within him, that he has a soul which is

part of Divinity, and that not to rise with it is a dis-
grace, then he is redeemed. This does not require any
creed-bound faith; rather it requires the consciousness
of that great Principle within and the desire to know
that Principle. When we know it, we become incapable
of harming or condemning any one. We find unity with
our bretheren and love for all human beings. Not only
that, our love extends to all things living and unliving.
We become more tender towards animals, more conscious of beauty in natural scenery and in surrounding
objects. They become living, they bring us rest.

A man bereft of inspiration, a man wholly dependent on material surroundings for his recreation, feels
lost if he is left alone. He is wholly dependent on outer
things. That one, however, who has found his access
within, when he is left alone not only does he not feel
lonely, he rejoices. The hours of solitude become rich
for him. No matter where we are placed or how we are
placed, if we are possessed of that inner awakening, we
are never lonely and our life is never unfruitful. It is
something we must try to develop and we do this by
cultivating the sense of divine Presence. When we deal
with material cold facts, we bring a living quality of
lightness and inspiration into them. This we must do
for ourselves; it cannot be mapped out for us by others.
It is our own attitude of mind which either gives us
access to these higher things, these subtler provinces, or
blocks our way. Let us perform our task with cheerful-
ness, light-heartedness and exuberance of spirit; then
perform the same task with depressed feeling, with a
morose and melancholy attitude; and compare the results. The work performed with the light of understanding and cheerful aspect, is invariably the better done.

Whenever we undertake anything with a sense of weight, doubt and despondency, we might as well not undertake it because it cannot be successful. If we carry life as though it were a dead weight, with unbelief and suspicion, the results will be negative; but if we undertake our tasks, our obligations and spiritual duties with faith, with divine inspiration, then not only shall we do our duties well, we shall draw constantly a fresh supply of life, a fresh supply of strength. What depletes man in his living is not so much overwork as lack of the sustaining Power. Excessive work may exhaust our energy and nervous force; but it is working without inspiration that breaks us. That is the real cause. It breaks the machine of our life. Our life's machine runs smoothly and successfully only when we oil it with love and inspiration. Let us remember this every hour that we live. If we carry with us this subtle sense of a higher Presence, not only when we are reading the Bible or praying before our altar, but at all times, and if we can open ourselves so that that great Power can flow through us, we shall never lack for anything. This is what the mystics call inspiration. By wiping out all selfishness, egotism and calculation from our hearts, we can make of ourselves open channels through which the divine Power can flow, just as it flowed thorough Valmiki. He did not know he was writing poetry, he had no desire to become an immortal personage, and because of that he became immortal.

Let us do our tasks without thought of self. Let us quiet our ambition. Ambition is a great drawback to true inspiration. Too much of it creates fever in the soul. When that fever of self-love and selfishness, that eager desire to be somebody, surges within us, it defeats our life and its purpose. Let us be silent like the flower, waiting patiently. Then inspiration will fall like the dewdrop, all unaware, and we shall see the fruition. The bud will come to blossoming, full of fragrance, full of beauty. And this is our life. If we have a task to perform, let us do it tranquilly. Whether the world notices us or not should not be our concern. Our consideration should be first and foremost what we are able to give, how fully we can give and how completely we can put ourselves aside. Out of this richness of gift we shall never fail to receive richness of inspiration and blessing.

G.

Man cannot truly enter into possession of his own latent possibilities until he has discovered and connected himself with his inner resources—until he has awakened his spiritual nature.

All the imperfection and limitation which we feel in our body and mind we can remove by not constantly thinking of this immediate, apparent, physical existence, but by joining our thoughts with the Higher Source, the fountainhead of life and energy. When we can remain focused there, we shall be able to go on doing our duties without feeling any reaction. That is one of the great secrets of the Indian Sages. Through the ages they have taught that man can make his work a recreation, that if he will connect himself with the Highest and keep his motive lofty, his work instead of exhausting him will bring him ever greater strength.

Paramananda

THE ETERNAL WAY
By Swami Paramananda

One single glimpse of Truth stands out like a beacon light. That is why those moments when we are capable of genuine spiritual vision are more precious than all the hours we may spend in study and theoretical speculation, and are sufficing to guide us through the periods of struggle when we do not know which way to go or what path to follow.

"Thou wilt show me the path of life. For with Thee is the fountain of life: in Thy Light shall we see light." In this mystic utterance lies an urge to men to turn their faces toward that Light which is unchanging and without which life is chaos and full of danger. Now there is not one single mortal who does not crave, desire and yearn for the Changeless. We may out of helplessness accept what we call the inevitable changes of existence, but in the soul of every creature is an inherent longing for the eternally abiding. It is this longing that the great souls of the world have tried to satisfy. Was not this the quest of the Lord Buddha? When his father strove to preserve him from contact with misery and place his feet upon what he hoped would be a smooth and comfortable road, another path opened out before him—a path that sooner or later opens out before everyone, because it cannot be hidden. Shocked by the knowledge of disease, death, pain and old age, he started forth to discover a condition beyond all chaos and affliction, and he found that happy "Paradise" and called it *Nirvana*. Many ignorant of its true nature, however, mistook it for an actual material realm. "Master," asked one of his disciples, "Is the promise of the happy region vain talk and a myth?"

"What is this promise?" asked the Buddha, and the disciple replied: "There is in the west a paradise called the Pure Land, exquisitely adorned with gold and silver and precious gems. There are pure waters with golden sands, surrounded by the pleasant walks and covered with large lotus flowers. There are singing birds whose harmonious notes proclaim the praises of religion, and in the minds of those who listen to their sweet sounds, remembrance arises of the Buddha, the law, and the brotherhood. No evil birth is possible there, and even the name of hell is unknown . . ."

"In truth," said the Buddha, "there is such a happy paradise. But the country is spiritual and it is accessible only to those that are spiritual . . ." "I understand," said the *savaka*, "that the story of the Western Paradise is not literally true."

"Thy description of paradise," the Buddha continued, "is beautiful; yet it is insufficient and does little justice to the glory of the pure land. The worldly can speak of it in a worldly way only; they use worldly similes and worldly words. But the pure land in which the pure live is more beautiful than thou canst say or imagine. However . . . he only can reach the happy land whose soul is filled with the infinite light of truth. He only can live and breathe in the spiritual atmosphere of the Western Paradise who has attained enlightenment. Verily I say unto thee, the Tathagata lives in the pure land of eternal bliss even now while he is still in the body . . ."

The hearts of the disciples had been enflamed with desire to find this beautiful country, and we can imagine how depressed they were when he told them it was purely of the spirit, just as we are depressed when the real Physician comes and tells us that the way out of our difficulties and tragedies lies within ourselves. We are most of us eager to set out on hazardous adventures for the sake of material reward, but when the real Voice tells us to look inward for our treasure, we feel helpless. We are willing to pay large fees to those who misguide us, but when the Voice of Truth tells us directly, "First seek ye the kingdom of God and its righteousness and all other things shall be added unto you," we call it vague and visionary. We prefer to follow the conflicting voices of the world until we fall down exhausted. Such is our logic.

"Seek ye first the kingdom of God . . . " That was Christ's teaching, you say. Of course it was; and not Christ's alone. It has been the message of all who stood for eternal Christhood. Only those understand it, however, who are willing to explore within. The Path of Life leads us within. Whether it is escape we are seeking from sickness or sorrow, or spiritual revelation, makes no difference. At every turn, invariably, it points the way inward, to the depths of our own being.

Our habit is, whenever we are molested by circumstances, to go to a person or a place in order to regain our peace and our bearing. These are people who shed healing balm; also there are places of spiritual fortification where the world's turbulent atmosphere does not enter. Often in such sanctuaries great healing will come upon one. These things are not impossible. But the real truth is, we must learn to walk on the Path of Life—of our own choice—voluntarily. It is not enough in a lifetime, to receive a spiritual experience accidentally, or at the hand of another. We should choose a definite path and walk that way.

There is such a thing as our becoming so involved in the life without, that our inner life sinks into nothing and seems almost like a myth. For instance, this idea that the kingdom of God is within us—what does it mean to most human beings? The average man, when he closes his eyes—as I have myself been told— and tries to concentrate his mind upon spiritual reality, sees absolutely nothing but darkness. There are those, however, who evolve something out of that darkness. The light of the soul bursts upon them—a way opens—a trackless path—following which they find not something imaginary, but that which is actual, definite. In saying this I do not mean definite in the sense of a chair or a tree or any material object, but none the less real.

Now when great Masters speak of this inner Paradise, this realm beyond disease, death and affliction, the soul of man cries out for it, but as soon as man is told that the way to it lies within himself, and that to tread it he must silence all that is restless in his nature, give up the crooked ways of the world and forget his eating, drinking, sleeping self with its egotistic feelings, he loses interest and turns aside. Sometimes it is necessary to forget all that we have learned.

Swami Vivekananda once said to a group of intellectuals who came to him full of pride in their worldly
knowledge and attainments: "Is there not enough water in the Indian Ocean for you to drown all these
things you have acquired? Forget your honors, diplo-
mas and credentials; then come to me and I will talk
with you." A very similar thing Christ said to the rich
man when he told him to sell all that he had in order to gain eternal life. The trouble is, we long to
find the blessed region, but at the same time we want
to cling to the things of this earth, even though they
may not be giving us any satisfaction, and so we keep
on revolving round and round our old circle of
thoughts and habits. We may talk all we please about
visions and revelations and religious experience, but
nothing can be ever really established within us until
we have proved it by our own inner, contemplative
trend of mind. Spiritual experience is not just a scrap
of paper you pick up somewhere and throw away again
after reading, nor it is a question of thoughts learned
from a Bible that you take down, dust, and put back
again upon its shelf. It is a question of following a
path on which these things—these great thoughts and
ideas—can be kept before you constantly,—a path that
can never be closed behind you, and upon which you
can help others to walk because you have found the
way to it yourself.

Do not think of this merely as a concept or an
intellectual venture. No—it is life itself; and life means
transformation—constantly letting go. When we walk
on one path we give up traveling on another. When
we travel on the inner road, naturally outer things fall
away. This question of renunciation has troubled many

people. It does not mean tearing from us things that we love and cling to. It means that they simply fall off from us because we are no longer interested. The fact is, there is too much renunciation from the surface. Man does not become free spiritually merely by spectacular renunciation of the external.

In ancient India, there was a king named Janaka. The average man thinks he has no time to give God because of his family, his duties, his obligations, but King Janaka who had all the affairs of a great state to attend to, yet found time for communion with Deity. This drew many holy men to his court to discuss with him concerning the deeper problems of existence. One day as he was engaged in a profound conversation with one of these ascetics, a messenger came in mad haste with the news that the palace was on fire and that there was great peril not only to the king himself but also to his priceless possessions. The ascetic who possessed only his loin cloth and a small bundle became very excited for fear that he should lose the little he had, but the king, absorbed in his thoughts of the soul, replied: "If the whole kingdom of Mithila should be burned to ashes, it would not alter anything that is mine." This is an illustration of what happens when one takes the spiritual course.

Here you may object. You may think that if you had an endowment or were rich and fortunate you also could sit down and think of spiritual things. I wonder if you would. If you do not do it now, you would not do it then. Often we think more of God when we are under strain and pressure than when we are not, though it should be just the other way. As a matter of fact, do we not always seek out the things that we love, and when we have time, do we not turn to them for recreation and refreshment? A man who has lower propensities turns to lower levels as soon as he has the opportunity, while men of higher type seek out the beautiful aspects of life to a greater or less extent, according to the degree of their experience and their capacity. The path of life that we follow,—narrow or broad, easy or hard, exalted or debasing—is as we have made it. There is, however, an eternal way which is one and the same for every human soul and those who follow that speak the same language, think the same kind of thoughts, and feel the same love in their hearts. That is the reason there is a kinship among spiritual men and women all over the world. There is no variation. It matters not that one person is born in America, another in England, and a third somewhere else. If they follow that path they will bear the same stamp of love—the eternal Principle. Love works everywhere,—under sordid conditions of life and in exalted moments. No one can alter it or its universal tongue. We talk about brotherhood, about a world that shall be free at last from wars, discord, unrest and unhappiness, but in order to find such a world, we shall have to learn to follow the path which alone leads to it.

Know this, my friends, if there is an urge, if there is something we feel within our soul, there is no barricade, there is nothing that can ever hinder us from attaining it. I have traveled and talked with people whose language I could not speak and who could not speak mine, yet we have understood one another. For there is a universal language, an expression that is unmistakable. The expression of love can never be mistaken anywhere. It is the one thing that does not fail, and I want to lay my emphasis on that. It is not by saying to you, "Follow this faith or this path," that you will immediately be enabled to find God. If it were so, all the world would be saved. People have tried that; they have even gone with sword and gun to convert the world. I prefer the instruction that Lord Buddha gave to his disciples, those whom he was sending out to mankind with his message. "Go forth," he said, "for the good of many and the happiness of many." That was indeed a beneficent thought to breathe into the hearts of men. Let concern for the individual be wiped out, let it be lost in the welfare of the whole. So shall we find our goal. Sometimes we find it when we are not seeking it at all, in fact when we have altogether lost concern for our own interest. I have witnessed cases of miraculous healing brought about by absorption in that which is exalted and exalting. In those moments of intense inspiration, all aches and pains were forgotten and fell away. It is like changing one's attitude, going from a lower region to a higher, so that one can breathe fresher air. Expert physicians frequently use this trick, when they prescribe a change, but the healing that I refer to is not due to some miracle that the doctors have performed, it is a miracle placed upon us by the Divine Hand, when we forget ourselves, our self-imprinted, self-cherished notions and turn within to the real values of life. That is why I say that the true path of life is the inner path. Without the inner life, no man can have any experience that amounts to anything. Without the inner life a man lives on the surface of existence. Sometimes we ask a friend to go for a drive. The scenery is beautiful, but our friend lacks the sense to see the beauty, and keeps up a constant conversation. This shows an impoverished type of consciousness. An individual of this type who has to be constantly entertained by somebody else's voice, with somebody else's thought, when is he going to seek refreshment within?

That inward refreshment we need in our modern life, and especially under the present terrible pressure of war and tragedy. Where else today shall we find it? Of course we are tremendously supplied with artificial means. Think of all the moving picture houses we have in every city, as well as countless other means of entertainment. Yet more and more as we are drawn outside ourselves, less and less do we feel the import, the vitality, the soul force which we must have to open for us the gate to the Land of Bliss. Kabir, the great mystic, says that it opens always through the touch of love. That is the secret of the trackless path. You are an intellectual being and no doubt you have tried many ways to open this gate. Everyone has. But one thing we have not tried, at least wholeheartedly—and that is the way of love. I can hear your answer: "Oh, but I have tried! I have heard that love heals; I have tried to be loving." Trying is one thing and actually loving is another. If you have tried a little and it has not worked, try harder. Suppose you find many obstacles rising before you, suppose you find people who are unloving and who excite those same feelings in you! All the more reason for you to bring forth what you possess within yourself. There is a reservoir in every man from which the soul may draw power and spiritual bounty. He cannot draw from it, however, if he is always reaching out into the external world.

At every hour of the day we must remind ourselves of the path leading within—the eternal path— and strive to cultivate the capacity, the resolution and the one-pointed purpose to follow it. This does not mean that we have to kneel all the time before the altar and pray, nor is it that we have to carry a Bible in our hand. But we do have to carry the essence of these things. The essence never leaves us, and wherever we are—at our homes or engaged in business—we can draw upon it for inspiration.

The point is, whether we talk about meditation or prayer, whether our religion is old-fashioned or new, it will have to be practical. It must enrich our lives now. Men and women of this world learn more by seeing one among themselves who has made a genuine success of his life than by all the preaching. A noble example stimulates the heart, and it is the heart that must be stimulated.

Defects and failures in others we should not think of. These things do not concern us. If we start with the idea of failure, we are going to fail. All the God-given power that we possess cannot save us if we are not conscious that we possess it. Make up your mind that you are going to succeed, not for the sake of self-gratification, but that you may become a channel for the Most High, and there will be nothing that can stand before the magnitude of such a thought.

All that is needed is sincerity of purpose and dedication of the life. These never fail to bring practical idealism. All men have tremendous zeal for what is practical, but the consciousness of men is not the same nor the means that they employ to attain their goal. Superficial means never bring lasting results. Whenever you strike a chord that is in tune with the people's interest, it will sound forth with tremendous volume. For instance, in this country if someone comes with a practical idea for making money, thousands will flock to him; while in India, the land of spirituality, if any one with the voice of truth proclaims: "I have found the way of eternity!" he will have even more followers.

"The good is one thing, the pleasant another. These two having different ends bind a man. It is well for him who chooses the good. He who chooses the pleasant misses his true end." Here sounds the voice of the sages of India; but other voices are loud and try to discourage us. "Only this life is real," they tell us. "Live in the senses and enjoy the present." Such advice may sound practical but there is no real logic behind it. People puffed up with worldly experience are not equipped to guide us on the path of truth. So long as we listen to these outer voices, we shall be unable to hear the true Voice or take the Hand which alone can lead us to the Light.

Let us then seek the inward way and become established on it. It matters not what religion we follow or what our chosen creed may be. These distinctions are fictitious. He who has entered the path of life finds that all religions lead to the same goal, and that goal is great oneness beyond all differences, unbroken bliss and the knowledge that is absolute and eternal.

ॐ

*M*en *may partition off their lands by measuring rods and boundary lines, but no one can so partition the all-embracing sky over the head. The indivisible sky surrounds all and includes all. So the unillumined man in his ignorance says that his religion is the only true one and that it is the best. But when his heart is illumined by the light of true Knowledge, he comes to know that above all these wars of sects and creeds presides the one Existence-Knowledge-Bliss Absolute. Whoever performs devotional exercises with the belief that there is but one God, is bound to attain Him.*

Sri Ramakrishna.

COSMIC CONSCIOUSNESS
By *Swami Paramananda*

uccess in spiritual study depends on how well we can fix and focus our mind, and upon the attributes of our mind. It is not just a mechanical practice—this mental focusing—a period of silence for the purpose of gathering together our forces, although the average person may look on it as such, nor is it the result of calculation or of how much intellectually we may know. It is a question of quality. If our mind is tranquil and receptive, if it possesses certain essential elements, then not only are we able to enter the realm of higher thought, but we may succeed in exploring there, in penetrating ever deeper and deeper into that kingdom. The intelligence, which is now ours, through which we are able to perceive the things of this world, that same intelligence, when properly unfolded, enables us to perceive the greater realities even as we now do the small and trivial objects of the sense plane. I must remind you of these facts in relation to our theme of Cosmic Consciousness. Within our own self, within our own being, we possess that which all great souls covet,—a light which illuminates everything and makes all things clear.

Very soon after I came to this country, Dr. Bucke's book on Cosmic Consciousness was published, and I remember what a tremendous sensation it cre-

145

ated. It contained examples of men who, to the author's mind, had touched this higher state of being, and I remember how people brought the book to me, a little skeptical, yet inclined to be interested intellectually and otherwise. Soon everyone was talking of Cosmic Consciousness, and it was not long before this country was overrun with psychologists and so-called "men of wisdom," who offered to sell it at so much a lesson. But Cosmic Consciousness cannot be bought in the marketplace: it is something we unfold.

When I say that we cannot buy Cosmic Consciousness in the marketplace, I do not mean that we cannot acquire it. Everyone knows what the word "cosmic" means—that which includes everything; therefore Cosmic Consciousness is that consciousness, possessing which, we come to possess the unlimited. The basic idea is this:

As normal human beings we are aware of certain things. Our knowledge may not be absolute, it may not be free from error, nevertheless we have within us the possibilities of a knowledge that is absolute. Our ordinary consciousness can be developed. The same mind, the same power, by means of which we know the lesser world, can be evolved so as to bring us in contact with the greater. It does not mean that suddenly we come upon or accidentally obtain something other than what we already have. It does not mean that, my friends. It means that what is already ours we unfold from within; but the instrumentality has to be suitable.

Thus, our mind, when clear, concentrated, unbiased and unmixed, is able to perceive things almost with prophetic vision, but when it is disturbed, agitated or clogged, everything appears to it as distorted. Great souls have often compared a troubled mind to a small body of water into which someone has thrown a stone, thereby stirring up the mud. When the mud is stirred up, naturally the water is no longer clear; nothing within it is visible, nor can one see the bottom. Just so is it with us when we keep on holding anxious thoughts: the whole surface of our mind is agitated and becomes incapable of reflecting the true Image. That is the reason why the average mind, which has the possibility of correct perception, is unable to perceive correctly, and that is why we need to look to the mind.

The Hindus have rather an extraordinary concept: they hold that within every human being there is a coiled up force which they call the *Kundalini*, the basic energy. When that is released, the individual finds himself in possession of a power that is inexhaustible. This power does not release itself by chance. In some cases, in fact in most cases, those who are conscious in a cosmic sense, seldom know that they possess it. Its coming is as natural and as spontaneous as is the opening of a flower when it blossoms. One is really not aware. There is no noise, no ostentation. On the contrary, the real unfoldment occurs when the individual is seeking nothing for himself. It is a very difficult subject to explain intellectually, because Cosmic Consciousness causes us to rise altogether away and aloof from ordinary concepts. It carries us to a province beyond the pale of human self-limitation and brings us face to face with realities which at the present moment we do not care to recognize or accept, although we may declare our faith in religion. Only when we have known, felt, seen and directly perceived are we convinced of all that pertains to the consciousness of the Self or what we call Higher Consciousness. In India they describe it by the Sanskrit term *Samadhi*. A man in that state becomes oblivious, often seemingly dead to, the physical, but completely aware of that loftier realm and its reality.

In that great Hindu classic, the Bhagavad-Gita, it is said: "That which is night to all beings, therein the self-subjugated remains awake, and that wherein all beings are awake, that is night for the knower of Self." In other words, on the sense plane where you find relentless activity and where people suffer and struggle and feel they know so much, from there the wise withdraw, because they see the futility of it all and are no longer interested. But in the spiritual realm, which seems to the ordinary human being divided from him as if by a veil, the wise are active and energetic. Some there are who, even when the whole world sleeps, remain wide awake engaged in thought and meditation. At the present moment our mind is so completely centered on the trivial and the petty that it does not care to find its access into the Vast and the Unbounded.

The thing is, we cannot be conscious of something that we do not want to be conscious of. There are many people who desire things out of curiosity. With the higher state of being, however, it is not a question of just wanting—as you would say, "I want wealth! I want power!" We have to have a profound yearning—we have to have the fitness. For according to the fitness, Cosmic Consciousness comes.

In India, the great psychologists worked out systematically and scientifically the connection of the mind with certain centers in the human body, which cause it to assume certain roles. As an example, when the mind is focused on lower centers, its tendency is food, drink, sleep, sense-pleasures. Perhaps we indulge in gossip, in all manner of things which have no importance, because our mind is stooping down to the level of these things. On the other hand, one who is highly cultured, who has more intellectual interests, will turn away from gossip and all such matters, for his mind has taken a different course. There is, however, a level higher than the intellectual and the aesthetic. There are individuals who live in a purely spiritual world. They like best to think on spiritual matters, to hear men talk about God and our connection with Him, and who appreciate and enjoy this deeper contact with as much keenness as the man bent on sense experience enjoys sense objects. They live in another atmosphere, that is all; their mind is connected with a higher center.

This does not mean that we can perform an operation and disclose this center here and that center there. These matters are subtle; they lie beyond the reach of ordinary methods. You may say, "I will not believe until I see." That is your great misfortune. The trouble is we want to prove spiritual truths by material means. They can be proved, but only through spiritualizing the mind, and that means individual effort, individual endeavor, individual practice, and dedication.

We have the power to change our mental focus. Mind forms habits; also it is very susceptible to outer influences—it takes their tincture. A piece of white cloth, if a corner of it accidentally drops into some dye, immediately assumes that color. So also with us. We come in contact with a man of genius and at once we take on the coloring of his mind. We hear him talk, receive his impression, as it were, and are given a tremendous stimulus. Similarly, when we associate with a man who is despondent or of evil propensities, if we are not positive enough, we take on his mental coloring. We can, however, become so strong, so fixed in the higher centers of our being, that nothing can impose its influence on us if we do not desire it. And how do we become strong? By thinking and rethinking and constantly thinking of that which is strong, spiritual and exalted. Only in this way can the mind be lifted—never accidentally.

We cannot say that anything is an accident. All the tragedies that are taking place in the world, if we have the power to analyze, do not take place because of accident. People mould their lives; they are constantly forming their own mental concepts, and these mental concepts grow ever more real and living and finally determine the state of their consciousness. Cosmic Consciousness is, for the one who experiences it, a stupendous reality. Our consciousness may now be full of error, of limitation, but when we make our connection, affiliate ourselves with the Unbounded, our mind becomes possessor in a definite way, of that which is inexhaustible.

Let us take an immediate case, one that is interesting because it illustrates so well a saying of a very great mystic, Jacob Boehme: "I am not collecting my knowledge from letters and books, but I have it within my own Self; because heaven and earth with all their

inhabitants and moreover God Himself is in man."
Let us take the case of Sri Ramakrishna. Sri
Ramakrishna used to say: "O mind, stay in your
own house—stay within your own dwelling! What
is the use of running hither and thither, searching,
and squandering your energy?" Of course, in the mystic sense, what he said was: "Don't have all this restlessness. Look within your own mind; there you will
find what you are seeking!" and he verified it.

There is, as I said, no accident. It may happen
that a person excited or enkindled may for an instant
arouse that divine energy within himself so that a
certain amount flows through him, but one who has
found his access into that higher realm experiences
this mighty power on all occasions. The reason we feel
impoverishment is because we have cut ourselves off
from that Source. We can make again our connection,
though not through mechanical means. Great souls
have done so, and what other souls have done, we
can do. It is all a question of valuation. What do you
love most? Mind follows the desire—upward or downward. It can become so attached to the lower centers
that it no longer perceives what is sublime and high.
It stands in its own light, so to speak. Light is always
coming from above, but we shadow it. The object that
we are trying to study, the problem we are seeking to
solve we obscure by our mental attitude. For instance,
a person with broken faith, bent down in tragic pos-
ture, wherever he looks he discerns only the shadow
of his own distorted self. When he lifts his head, however, when he changes his mental gaze, at once he
beholds everything in the light.

Perhaps you are skeptical. You might think: "He

is trying to give us a little sophistry." It is not soph-istry; it is fact. Our mind can lift us way up to heaven and also it can cast us down to the most hideous state of suffering. Everything exists in the mind. It is not, I repeat, through accident that we find our ex-altation, happiness and fulfillment, our plenitude and our strength—never through accident. It is through the continued control and direction of the mind. There-fore, from every point of view, the study of the mind is the most vital study for man.

Knowledge is what we all want to acquire. The business man wants it, one who desires to advance along any line wants it, because knowledge is power. But where lies the key to knowledge? The only key which we hold and can handle is the key of our own mind. If the mind is clogged, undecided, dimmed, then we never find that key, and the door of knowl-edge remains closed to us.

Among the Indian legends there is a parable illu-strating this. It concerns the Great God Shiva and His consort, the Great Goddess. As these two were passing over the earth, they beheld a wretched mor-tal who, through ill fortune and his own attitude, had lost his faith in everything. With head bowed, he was walking along in the depths of despair. According to the parable, the Goddess—tender, merciful, said to Lord Shiva, the One who does good to all beings: "O Lord, why do you not remove this person's misery?" And He said: "I cannot." And she said: "That is im-possible; you can do anything." "No," He replied, "mortals sometimes stand in their own light. I will prove it to you. This man is seeking wealth. Very well, I shall place a bag of gold in his path." Imme-

diately a bag filled full of golden coins was laid before his pathway. But he, disgusted with everything,
suddenly closed his eyes, saying: "I do not even want
to look on this wretched world!" and so he passed by
the gold without seeing it. In the same way, do we
not often pass by opportunities, owing to our mental
blindness and distorted notions?

When we are unaware of our divine heritage, the
outside world plays havoc with us. For instance, hold
the thought that you are evil and see how much evil
will fall upon you. Take an attitude of dejection and
note how quickly the whole of your mental horizon
will become darkened. Then enter the arena of life
with another point of view,—with hope, aspiration and
faith, and observe how all things will pave the way
toward that higher realization. The fact is, we see this
world as we allow ourselves to see it. But what makes
one see it as ugly, another as beautiful? Why is it
that a great personage in his moment of exaltation
exclaims: "Verily, this whole world is full of God!"
while in the same spot someone else will cry: "This
world holds nothing but evil?" Perhaps we can explain
it in this way—when the mind is turned downward,
then a man perceives nothing but the sordid facts of
life; he sees reality only in the small, impermanent,
changing, shifting conditions; while the mind that is
directed upward is more conscious of what is beneficent, abiding, and finds reality there.

Here you will say: "How can we deny the things
we see?" You cannot deny them; you can learn to see
them differently. It is not that we have to struggle to
deny, we simply change our angle of vision. We cannot center our consciousness on the finite and the

petty and at the same time hope for the unfoldment of that which relates us to the Infinite. There lies our trouble today: we want everything and we are willing to sacrifice nothing. Even the things that are not good for us, the bondages, even these we are not willing to give up. How then can we hope for Cosmic Consciousness?

The cosmic energy, when it is set into motion, breaks all barriers; it awakens us from slumber; it quickens the spirit of man. And it achieves these results silently. Never in my life have I heard so much noise about Cosmic Consciousness as during these last few years in America. Those who really find their access into this exalted state express it quite differently. In India, a land where people frequently have attained it, you hear very little talk about it. It is so stupendous, vast, that there is no language to describe it. Walt Whitman says: "When I undertake to tell the best, I find I cannot; my tongue is ineffectual on its pivots; my breath will not be obedient to its organs: I become a dumb man." The Vedic Upanishads describe it as being "beyond mind and speech." This does not mean that men of vision lack the power of expression, it means that as we recognize Infinitude we cannot define it by words. We may sing hymns and formulate speculations, yet it remains ever untold.

According to Sri Ramakrishna, this consciousness can be reached only when the individual ego, the self, is put to sleep. The thought of this may frighten you, just as some people are frightened when they came into Sri Ramakrishna's presence, for he lived practically in that transcendent state, and even when he came down to the ordinary sense levels, he brought with him the atmosphere of that vaster realm. Do not, however, think that this made him unfit for everyday living. It did not. And in this connection let me give you a story:

Once a young disciple came to stay with Sri Ramaskrishna and, as was the custom, they went together to bathe in the Ganges. The devotee took with him a water jar and a towel, but left them behind. On their return, Sri Ramakrishna asked him what he had done with them. He said: "I forgot them. My spiritual devotions drove them completely out of my mind." He thought this would make a tremendous impression. But that great saint, Sri Ramakrishna, replied: "You forgot? For many years I have lived in a condition of spiritual ecstasy, at times losing all physical consciousness, yet I have never forgotten a single thing."

These words are a warning. Many believe that when they grow a little visionary, absent-minded, or unregardful of what is immediately before them, it is a sign of inner progress. Let me tell you this: when there is actual progress, your perceptions grow keener, your commonsense more uncommon and your attitude toward the world around you, a thousand times more wakeful than before.

We must never confuse high realization with the egotistic sense. We must find the true Self. But that true Self, what is it? Is it the body? Is it these senses? Or is it the eyes, ears, mind, brain? Our present feeling of self-importance is an egotistic notion and instead of helping us is more likely to hinder. Egotism stands between man and God, and that is why Sri Ramakrishna declares that until that is wiped out, man cannot make his contact with Divinity. Often in the Scriptures we find utterances which appear

like direct contradictions. For instance, that Christ
note—"Thy Will be done!"—seems the opposite of His
statement—" I and my Father are one." The first signifies surrender, the second, self-recognition; yet we
must realize that both mean the same thing. We surrender to the Highest and finally come to identify
ourselves with that Highest. In neither case is there
room for the little self, the ego, the "I and mine."
That consciousness is altogether eliminated. We give
up everything and find at every turn an inexhaustible
Source from which we can draw.

Why has the average mind so little strength? Because it has weakened itself. It should be like a single
thread; instead, it has become like a lot of fibers. We
can, however, gather up these fibers of our mind—our
poor, distracted mind—going this way and that way in
countless different directions, and draw them into one;
just as sometimes we put together many pieces of
thread and twist them into a rope that is gigantic in
its power of resistance. At the present moment our
mental forces are divided and dissipated; we can command only a small portion of them; but when they
are made into one whole, twisted and combined like
a rope, they become for us a unit of tremendous
power.

If at the present moment this seems to be beyond
you, do not allow yourself to be dejected. Do not say:
"It is not for me; I never can hope to accomplish it."
We must guard our mind against this tendency to go
downward. Going downward does not mean necessarily indulging in sense pleasure or any definite form of
evil. It may mean dejection or any negative tendency
brought about through brooding or self-pity.

Lift the mind up! Even though it may fall down many times—lift it up! The Hindus feel that one of the best means for doing this is association with the holy. First, though, we must learn to know who is holy and who unholy. When we come in contact with men who are dedicated, consecrated, we find a tremendous amount of solace: the strong focused atmosphere which they create is very, very helpful. We must learn to create such an atmosphere. If instead of spending our leisure hours talking about our little failures and successes, our triumphs and disappointments, we would turn our thoughts into an entirely different channel, we would form a new world for ourselves. This may happen through necessity, because a man cannot keep his head and meet the many problems which confront him, unless he learns to draw from that unbounded Consciousness which alone can shed light upon his path. Man may possess wealth, he may have power, he may have all these things, but to what avail if he lacks wisdom, if he lacks the one Light? India realized this and that is why in that land there are so many who are willing to give up everything in order to find the light. It has become their passion. As Dr. Bucke says: "There is a mental state so happy, so glorious, that all the rest of life is worthless compared to it, a pearl of great price, to buy which a wise man willingly sells all that he has. This state can be achieved."

There comes a time when fervor like this enters into our soul. Then we cannot be contented with small spiritual gains. We seek and seek with ever greater yearning and concentration. The matter is, once we have had the real taste of spiritual bliss we

can never abandon our quest. That is why truth seek-
ers are so oblivious of all else and at times appear as
it were intoxicated or mad because they have no other
thought but of their chosen ideal. This tremendous
zeal and one-pointedness of purpose quicken their intuition—a most valuable asset always to the attainment
of Cosmic Consciousness.

Someone asked Sri Ramakrishna how Christ was
able to endure the actual physical pain on the cross
as he did. He answered it through the following parable: When the coconut is unripe the whole thing—
kernel, pulp and shell—is bound together so that it is
very difficult to separate them, but after it ripens the
kernel separates itself from the external shell. They
become like two different objects. Finally one rolls
freely within the other and can be detached from it
without any difficulty. Same way was it with Christ
or with one who has attained the Supreme Consciousness. His soul life is ever detached from the physical
and therefore he can so easily transcend the afflictions
of body and mind and this is truly the most vivid picture of Cosmic Consciousness.

Intellectually we may understand it to a certain
extent, but intellectual understanding does not save us
from suffering or sorrow caused by the onslaught of
the world. We are like the parrot who is able to sing
sacred songs and repeat holy names till the cat goes
after him. Then he forgets his texts and can only
scream in his own parrot tongue. So do we forget,
until our knowledge of that great Immensity has become real. Then actually we enter that realm and our
entire being is transformed. Finding That which is
vast and unlimited and knowing our connection with

It, all fear of loss is done away with forever.

Who can give an idea of this tremendous subject? Speech melts into nothingness. Therefore to express it, we have to reverse the usual order. Silence instead of speech; humble living instead of boisterous, restless seeking. "How are we going to reach this?" the restless world will ask. There comes a stage in our struggle when spontaneously we grow silent. Have you never found yourself sitting watching a sunrise or sunset—all alone, quiet—the whole world forgotten? And at that time did not something seem to unfold? Was there not something born in you?—a different kind of experience, an oblivion, a self-forgetfulness—a forgetfulness of all your surroundings, so that nothing existed but a reality which you could not define or describe? Well, just in this way, the great Ideal, the great Power is born within the soul, and once we have contacted it, never more can we be bound. A passage from the Sacred Upanishad tells us that: when that unfolds within us, everything becomes clear, all the knots of our mind and heart are cut asunder, all our doubts are destroyed. Everything that is dark or confused in our life or the life of the world vanishes when we come face to face with that great Light.

Look for it! hope for it! and never stop until you have found it. Shall we be satisfied with a partial glimpse, partial knowledge, partial understanding, when there is this craving for fullness of life, and of happiness. Other things do not matter. We must not accept any defeat. We must go on until we come to That which illumines the individual existence—until we come into the full glow of that mighty Effulgence.

When this great light bursts forth upon our soul it

transforms our life and our entire consciousness expands with a newness of vision and aspiration which cannot be described by mere words. It is a thing to be known, it is a thing to become. It is indeed the fulfillment of the great Vedic utterance: "He has become It." No longer can our life be severed even for an instant from that overwhelming reality which is ever present, which is all in all, without which there is no life, there is no consciousness, there is no existence.

G_n

Where is this consciousness? Inside. But where inside? It is centered in the heart, not the brain. A man may have his brain injured, still his consciousness continues, although his mind may be deranged; but injure the heart and at once consciousness leaves the body. This shows that the chief seat of consciousness is in the heart.

Swami Ramakrishnananda

PRACTICE OF DIVINE PRESENCE
By Swami Paramananda

*Let us lift our inmost thoughts and prayers to that One
who resides within us and watches over us all—whose
love is unfailing, whose protection is unfailing.*

*Let us with all the strength of our being, with all the
power we posses, visualize that one.*

*Let us make His Presence definite, real, that we may
derive great benefit through our prayers, through our
spiritual communion,*

*May that infinite, all-abiding Spirit—our Father, our Mother,
Friend, our eternal Companion—manifest Himself
within us in a conscious way, and bestow upon us His
blessings in such a tangible manner, that we shall
realize His Presence and our lives may become
full of bounty, of strength, and of divine reality.*

*May He, the All-abiding, surround us with His unfailing
love and keep us ever and ever in peace.*

T here is nothing greater than to possess the joy, the peace of God within our soul. There are times when we feel this nearness of God more definitely than at other times, so definitely

in fact, that it leaves no question or doubt in our mind.
Life flows beautifully and we are aware of the blessing of
it. Then again that blessing disappears and a cloud seems
to fall. We blame ourselves for this, we blame circumstances, regrets overpower us and we are weighted with
a sense of self-depreciation.

Now is there no way that we can avoid these moments? If there is, we should seek it with unwavering
determination, because they constitute for us greater
tragedies than loss of material possessions. How can we
make that Divine Presence abiding?

Here you may object that for the majority of people
the idea of Divine Presence has no meaning. I think
everyone has an innate feeling for that Presence. Do we
not cultivate a sense of presence in the case of people
we love dearly? How often we preserve a photograph
of the living and of those who have passed away. We
feel that it creates at once a sense of nearness. The
reason I bring this point out so strongly is because often
we do not understand the ways of spiritual culture, spiritual practice and processes. There was a time when anything pertaining to the spiritual was neglected by the
intellectual mind as superstition, without ever analyzing
it. Yet, as I say, we never condemn when we find someone trying with definiteness, by means of a picture or
symbol, to visualize the memory of one he loves. He
even places flowers as an offering to the loved one. In
the same sense, the lovers of Truth, of God, seek to
create definiteness in their relation with the Ideal.

Anything that reminds us of Divinity, whether it
be man or woman, tree or stars, or beautiful scenery, is
blessed. The whole religious history of mankind
centers around the places of pilgrimage which mark the

starting point of man's spiritual ventures. The Bo Tree, beneath whose branches the Lord Buddha found the great Truth, the *Nirvana*,—that tree is preserved, or the place where it once stood. The *Panchavati*, where Sri Ramakrishna used to sit in meditation, draws thousands of pilgrims who come to touch the very dust of that spot, because they think something holy is there. Man wants to connect himself with anything no matter how concrete, even with a little speck of dust, that is associated with a place of attainment, in the hope that there may be some lingering perfume of the Presence. We long to find a point of definiteness and relate ourselves to it.

This tendency to visualize a living presence long after the passing away of a holy saint is not only pronounced among Hindus and Buddhists but among all the devout souls of the world.

In the year 1911, it was my great privilege to witness the outpouring of devotion at the Shrine of St. Francis of Assisi. Definite contact with the spirit of holiness and godliness is the constant craving of those souls who want to commune, who want to walk, talk and live with what is generally supposed to be unseen and unattainable.

There must be some way to create this definiteness. In India, people who seek it turn to spiritual men and women—not to those who may have excellent credentials for their learning, but rather to those who have attained, who emanate a Presence. Herein lies the secret of spiritual contact.

"The Light Divine within is obscured in most people. It is like a flame in a cask of iron. No gleam of light can shine through. Gradually by purity and unselfishness we can make that obscuring medium less and less dense, until at last it becomes as transparent as glass." I give this wonderful thought by Swami Vivekananda, because there are some who say, "If there is a Divine Presence why do we not see It? Since we do not see It, we cannot believe in It." That seems to them to be conclusive evidence that It does not exist. It only means that they have lost the sensitiveness which would enable them to hear the voice of God when in the hour of despair they long to hear It, or even to listen for It in the silence of the soul.

How sweet is the sound of silence!
How tender is its touch!
How fragrant is its breathing!
How lovely is its form!

"That is foolish!" the average man will reply. "How can there be sound in silence?" Silence is deafening to some people; others find in it nothing at all. That is why we so often reject this most vital issue of life. Who among us, when beset by difficulties, turns in the silence to that abiding Presence,—to that One who can always comfort us and bring us solace? Rather our first instinct is to seek human aid. We go to this man or that, but often he only increases our trouble, for his own heart is full of doubt and confusion.

Gradually by experience we learn that we have to detach ourselves from the earthly. Every man needs to do this, but it cannot be done at once. I am not going to prescribe any special form of practice—that is something that must be evolved through the individual soul. Each human being has his own way of approach. Perhaps one has excessive power of devotion, while another has the power to withdraw from noise and retire within his own being. We all have our special province, and it is for us to recognize it and search for it. No one can force us. There are many people, faithful to their own religion, to their creed and church, who try to force their beliefs upon their children. Often, however, they bring about an opposite result. During the long years of my stay in this country, I have found young men and women in the Occident who do not want even to hear the word, God. Is this not a strange psychology!

But what is there in a name, a creed, the crust of dogma? Our great Master, Sri Ramakrishna says, "The calendar predicts so much rain in the rainy season, but can you produce a single drop from it by squeezing it?" All that is sacred to us in the form of books and bibles and relics and ritualism does not produce any effect upon us unless through our vital faith, through our power to make living the Divine Presence. The question is— how may we practise that Presence? This is what I want to bring to you.

There is no normal person who is not always seeking companionship. Our whole life we are practising companionship with people, ideas and ideals, according to the trend of our thoughts. But the eternal Companion we fail to realize. Life itself seems to stand in the way. Material burdens, overwhelming thoughts of care,— everything comes to try us, until the mind, the heart, the brain,—the entire physical being seems devoid of light. How may we counteract these conditions? The only way is to bring in another current of thought. And how may we do that? By becoming childlike in our simplicity. A man may be very famous, a great intellectual figure, but no matter what he is or who he is, when he stands before that eternal Being, all his self-importance vanishes and he becomes like a little child. This seems to be the definite step we have to take for the practice of the Presence of Divinity.

In childhood you lie upon your mother's breast or in your father's arms and you never question if your parents will protect you. You know they will. But as you grow older, you lose that sense of protection, you worry, you do not trust people. In that great, eternal Presence, likewise, no questionings arise; all sense of untimely old age leaves you, and you no longer feel that you stand alone with no one to aid you. You know that you are in the keeping of an invincible Power and have nothing to fear. He will take care of you as He has always done. The real sun dissolves the mist, the fog and all the elements that have enshrouded us and robbed us of our courage. So it is that when we have found the true, the definite way of invoking that Presence, our worries, misgivings, disappointments and fears all vanish at once. It is not a matter of theory. Such fulfillment is not born out of theory. It begins with practice, and we start to realize it as soon as our minds are made over in the right direction.

Genuine spirituality is the emancipation of consciousness from all these material things. How wonderful to be able to retire within one's own Soul! We often say, "I want a time of rest. I want to be alone." Yet how seldom we take the opportunity. When we have the chance to relax, to think, to commune with our higher being, with God, Truth, we begin to plan how to fill our time. We create new fetters, new engagements. Our habits of living have become very complex, and until we can simplify we must endure the results of our chaotic mentality, for God will not interfere with our freedom. He gives us mind and body and it is for us to choose what line we want to follow.

Epictetus tells us, "When you have shut your doors and darkened your room, remember never to say that you are alone, for you are not. God is within, and your genius is within; and what need have they of light to see what you are doing?" This is a very significant thought. If you will always remember that God stands by, the inspector of whatever you do with your body or soul, you will never blunder through your prayers or in your actions, and you will have God abiding with you. That is one of the most wonderful things we learn from the person and example of Sri Ramakrishna. He did not pretend. He practised the Divine Presence. He did only that day after day.

Once a learned man came to question him, as a pupil would come to a teacher, expecting him of course to answer anything he might ask. But on this particular occasion Sri Ramakrishna could not answer. He said, "My friend, I do not understand it. Mother," (he called the Divine One "Mother" like a little child), "Mother does not seem to speak through me today." What an extraordinary thing! Where now shall we find any man with public reputation, any doctor or teacher, who would make such an admission? On the contrary, whatever we might ask of such a one, he would give an answer. But Sri Ramakrishna could not answer because the Mother did not speak through him. It is a lesson for us all. If men remained silent except when the great Voice spoke through them, how silent the world would be! What peace would come! The entire conflict would cease, since no one would speak until he was in tune with the eternal Source. If even a small portion of humanity would practise this, it would alter the destiny of mankind.

What is the cause of our present destiny? What is creating this confusion? Is it not due to the fact that we are trying to settle our problems by the sole aid of our arrogant, greedy, noisy, confused self? If we would but once close the avenues of our being to the outside world, to all the noises that create this chaos, the turning within, would call on the One Guardian to decide all our issues, everything would be altered instantly. We may not believe in miracles, but a miracle would take place at once. We are, however, fainthearted. We pretend to follow a creed, we are not afraid to die on the battlefield or go before a cannon, yet we are not courageous enough to follow the path of Christ or of Buddha. Lately we have read of suicide squads—men who give their lives to accomplish some desperate military purpose. Thousands have volunteered in such service. So you see it is not that we lack heroism but that our heroism is misdirected. Our life is God-given, and as soon as we realize that God-given life, that abiding Presence within, we become aware that our destiny is concerned with something more than passing human affairs. Many men have taxed their brains with human problems, yet have been unable to solve them. In fact, their efforts seem only to muddle them more and more.

I speak to you from my heart. Why not seek another guidance? Are you not tired of following things that fetter you and rob you of your aspirations? Why not make a change and investigate your *spiritual* sphere? Is this not logic? Will it not benefit you? Leaving aside the aspect of idealism, I think it is needful for physical well-being. We live a very tense, nervous existence, our minds are scattered and our habits have become so involved that we have vital need for a balancing factor in our life. Do not take my word for this, or the words that are written in books. Use your own common sense, as well as the rationalism and the spiritual vision you may possess. Try this inward turning for two or three days and you will have a more definite understanding concerning it.

Spirituality, as I have said, is not anything that can be imposed upon you or that you can impose upon others. If, however, you are yourself inclined to spiritual living, you are bound to encourage others through your life and being. Our greatest service to our fellowmen is the radiation we bring. You cannot hide your light under a bushel. If you possess it, it will be self-evident. No one can contact you without being conscious of it. He may not know just what it is that he feels, but he will say, "I wish I were like that man. I wish I had his mind, his courage, his character, his inward peace." When the iron cask becomes like glass, men can perceive these attributes shining through us. When it is dense, nothing can shine through it. Then we do not see anything. We are confused and bring our confusion into the world. The practice of the Divine Presence does away with this.

There is a guide within. Books, bibles, and great personalities through their utterances, through the radiation of their lives, create the stimulus. It is for us not merely to recognize that these ideals exist and have existed, but to keep them alive and bring them into manifestation through our own endeavor. Just as we make efforts in other directions, same way we can cultivate spiritual habits which once established will be of unspeakable blessing. Men talk of the essence of

Christian life. What does it imply? That we look to God in all our thoughts, words and actions, unto none else. Those who have learned to find their serenity in that divine Providence, their nature becomes living.

In seeking that great Presence, man has built temples and churches and cathedrals and beautiful shrines. He has lavished upon them gold ornaments, jewels and riches, thinking that because he has spent so much upon them, God must be there. Sri Ramakrishna, however, summed it all up in a significant answer he gave to the owner of the temple where he worshipped. This devotee, Mathur Babu, was berating the Divine Mother for permitting certain valuable ornaments to be stolen from the sanctuary. "My son," said Sri Ramakrishna, "what are these jewels to the Great Mother? Everything is Hers."

Do not conclude from this that I am urging you to do away with material worship. What I am trying to show you is that we should never take a step, should not walk, talk, eat or sleep or perform any other act, unless we have a sense of that Presence within us. Herein lies the safety of man. By even trying to follow this practice, we lessen the chance for accidents and minimize the misery in the world.

It is the thought of Divinity that brings the Presence of Divinity. Therefore in order to counteract repellant influences and create an atmosphere worthy of the Divine, we should make ready the place that we have chosen to perform His worship. In outer life when we have an honored guest, we cause our house to shine, we fill it with flowers, fragrance, and other lovely things, in order to give an impression of welcome. So it is that if we want the most beloved Guest of all, the most

Beautiful of all beings, we must make ready for Him with loving care; we must prepare a dwelling, a sanctuary, a throne—prepare it with all our heart, with such concentrated feelings, such dedication and true devotion, that it will be fit to receive Him.

God is love and love is God. Before realizing the Presence of the Divine we have difficulty in loving someone who is not loving, but after that realization we can say with Kabir, "I have attained the unattainable and my whole life has become colored with the color of love." It does not matter if you call yourself Hindu, Christian or Buddhist. Names are nothing. God is no respector of names and creeds. When you go to heaven you will not be recognized by these labels. The one thing that is recognized everywhere is love. That is the real creed, the real religion, the real Presence. Those who have not the presence of love in their souls do not know what it is to enjoy the Presence of Divinity. St. John says, "If a man says, I love God, and hateth his brother, he is a liar; for he that loveth not his brother whom he hath seen, how can he love God whom he hath not seen? And this commandment have we from him, that he who loveth God love his brother also." Therefore, strive to manifest this love. Manifest it within the sanctuary of your soul.

I share with you these thoughts, that every one of us may become inspired to strive for that inner life without blemish. I do not say that it is always easy. Circumstances may stand in our path to defeat us, but no matter how many times we fall down, let us rise again and work with a greater fervor than before. It is our mission in life to establish more firmly in our heart that Divine Presence. For if we carry it now, we shall carry it even when we leave our body.

Let us, therefore, in this hour of silence and sanctity, lift our whole being, our inmost secret feelings, to that One who is the Guardian, the presiding Deity, that He may sanctify everything through His Presence, that He may bless our life, our thought, and all the things we do and hope to do.

He is the Soul of our soul, the Light of the universe. May our whole life be lighted up through His light and be consecrated unto Him.

O Thou beneficent Spirit,
Thou art our tender Mother, our eternal, protecting
    Father!
Thou art our Friend and Companion!
Thou art All in All!
Lead us by Thy compassionate hand, for Thou art our
    strength.
Let us never fail or falter.
Guide us that our hearts may be filled with Thy light—
    Thy light of love—
And may we never be without Thy tender Presence.
Peace, peace, peace be unto us and to all living beings.

THY WILL BE DONE
By *Swami Paramananda*
*(An address delivered by the Swami at the Temple
of the Universal Spirit, Ananda Ashrama, California)*

e have here, in this subject of surrender one of the grandest of themes, found in practically all spiritual records both ancient and modern, and possessing a universal appeal. Naturally at once you connect it with your Christian Bible, beginning with the many sayings in the Old Testament, and finally given in the words of the great Master, Christ. But as we turn the pages of the scriptures and great Bibles of the world, everywhere we come across it in one form or another. It is a universally accepted principle, a grand, magnificent concept, holding before man the ideal that he should at every turn learn to submit his will, his power, and all that he calls his own, to God, the Giver of all good, and thus he may be secured in his actions, his thoughts, and in whatsoever may be his undertakings.

We can never submit our will to the Divine will, however, so long as we think we have greater wisdom than the Divine. That is one of the troubles with the world today—it has thought it could do things better than God could do them. What we call our modern civilization, with all that that includes, is an illustration of this. Therefore it is no wonder that we have so much loss and confusion, unrest and lack of peace, since this conflict first exists in our own mind.

173

It avails little or nothing if a man merely pretends that he surrenders everything to God, saying with his lips: "Thy Will be done!" as from our infancy we have heard preachers proclaim from the pulpit, and as we in our turn have taken up the refrain and given it out. It is something more than mere speaking. Words alone do not make one submissive to the Divine Will, and so long as we have even a shadow of doubt in our mind as to Its nature and our relation to It, we shall be unable to make It a reality in our life.

"If I give over my will to the Great Will," you may ask, "shall I be deprived of my happiness? Will there be for me as much of good, security and protection as there is now? Why should I take the risk?" These questions naturally come to our mind, but we must remember that surrender to God is not just an intellectual concept to be discussed and analyzed, or an ethical subject to calculate about, as to whether we should submit or we should not; it is a fact that grows upon us as we are able to perceive that the Divine Will is the most potent power and the only safe shelter for us in this entire universe. For this reason, we naturally turn to It as our understanding increases, instead of morbidly accepting It after we have been defeated by life and therefore feel that there is nothng else left for us to do.

There was a time when modern man was inclined to think that spiritual surrender was only for the negative, weak individual. The manly man, the intelligent, enterprising and capable man, why should he lay down his will? But surrender is not for the weak, and also I want to add here: it is not for the coward. Surrender calls for heroism. This may sound incongruous, because we think that the one who puts up his stubborn self-will, and fights, represents the strong type of manhood. In the final analysis, however, we find that his strength is only on the physical basis and is not anything we can depend on or that endures. It is not the strength of the Christlike, of those who in all circumstances stand up and face what human beings call "insurmountable difficulties," with never a complaint.

Let me read some of the great saying from the Christian Bible. The Christ said: "Whosoever shall do the Will of my Father Which is in heaven, the same is my brother and sister and mother." And again, "for I have not spoken of myself but the Father which sent me, He gave me a commandment, what I should say, and what I should speak . . . The word which ye hear is not mine, but the Father's Which sent me."

How it makes one think of Sri Ramakrishna! Once a man came and asked Sri Ramakrishna to instruct him. The Master tried to speak, but for some reason or other the words would not come, and he explained that he could only bring himself to speak when he had the consciousness of the divine voice speaking through him—not otherwise. What a standard! What an ideal! If even for a single day we should all put into practice not opening our lips unless we had the incentive and urge from within, what a wonderful change would come upon this world! We would, of course, talk much less, but whatever we did say would be of tremendous value to ourselves and to our fellows.

You can see that such an attitude of mind is not based upon a negative principle. It requires an infinite amount of moral courage, feeling and faith. It means that a man grows from within out, *from within out*, instead of trying to grow from without in, as we do now.

Man today notices whether or not his body is becoming stouter and stronger, and if he finds that through any mishap it is not, he immediately takes outer measures to increase its efficiency and power. But what is he doing inwardly to enhance his spiritual growth? When he is thwarted by the chaos around him, he gives up and accepts the confusion, because his outer horizon is limited and he does not know what the Divine Will is or how to turn to It. Now this condition can be counteracted, but only as he learns to seek within his own soul, and that means that his turbulent outer nature has to be silenced. The thing is, that as long as we believe we can do better and know better than God Himself, the idea of surrender will be far from us.

More cleverness—for a long time this has been our standard. Where has it brought us and what has man obtained through his cleverness—tell me that? Today I can speak very frankly because you are thinking along these same lines. Man has set his own traps, has created entanglements, mental worries and unhappiness for himself and for the world, yet now he does not know how to get free from them; he is unable to find any solution. He might turn within, but unfortunately he has been nurtured with the thought that the idea of submission to the Divine Will is a weak, old-fashioned idea, and is not for the practical province of mankind.

One of the most hopeful factors in the makeup of present-day humanity is its admiration for greatness. We admire a great character. Of course, sometimes our admiration is a little like that of the critics at Bernard Shaw's play, who were reluctant to pass any judgment till they knew who was the author. That is often our standard of judgment. Did a famous man do it? Then it must be good. Until a man has been accepted by the world, though he may be a towering genius, we hesitate to accept him. We do, however, have a desire to recognize what is great, and that at least is something in our favor. For instance, today the whole world, even including those who are most conventional, admits that Gandhi is a great man. Why? He goes practically unclad, and in many ways lives contrary to our accepted mode of living. He is not a militant general; he is not a diplomat in the ordinary sense; he is not a man who is striving to build up power for himself or to gain personal name and fame. What then is the source of his strength, and how can he dare in the face of all adverse thoughts and standards, put into practice the concept that anything and everything can be solved by a man when he submits himself to God? How often do you hear of a leader in politics or human society saying, "I am puzzled; I must seek the answer through prayer"? Does it not remind you of Christ when He retired to the Garden at the time He was face to face with His most terrible ordeal? Why did He not seek to organize an army? There were friends. Why did He not seek human aid? Human aid! He did not even pray to His Heavenly Father to send Him protection. He had only one desire—how he might find out clearly and without bias the Will of the Father, with no element of conflicting thought anywhere. What a strength! That is the reason why I say that surrender is not for the coward.

You and I have been brought up with the idea that to submit the will is to accept defeat, and that it could never be the way of one who is strong and clever with plenty of red blood in his veins. The few who have said "Thy Will be done" and have lived up to their

words, we have regarded as fools—and so is Christ regarded according to the standard of modern life. I am
only saying what you already know. There have even
been plays written to show what would happen to any
man who tried today to follow in the footsteps of
Christ. He would almost surely be arrested and would
finally land in an insane asylum, of which we have
plenty.

Man's will and the Divine Will are in clash, and
that is the reason why man is as backward as he is. It is
a blessed thing that at least he possesses the instinct
which causes him to recognize the possibility of surrender, and inclines him to open his heart when he actually sees someone, like Gandhi, who is achieving victory through this means.

"I can of my own self do nothing: as I hear, I judge:
and my judgment is just; because I seek not mine own
will, but the Will of my Father Which hath sent me."
What a great vision for a man to carry!—Christ knew
that to increase one's strength one should depend upon
the Source of strength and not merely on one's own
cleverness, shrewdness or physical valor.

Today we are going through a struggle, unmistakable. It is no imagination. Every one of us is called
upon to meet some phase of difficult adjustment. We
have spent many, many sleepless nights trying to solve
the problem, trying to find a clue. Have we found anything? On the contrary, the minds of most men have
become more confused, less clear, enshrouded with
greater doubt, therefore with greater weakness, than ever;
because when doubt enters, one always is made weaker.
Should we not pause, then, when everything else has
failed, and try at least to analyze our position in order to

discover if there is not some way we can unite our frail mind and all our mental and material forces under the One Great Power Whom we call "Father, Mother, Friend, Great Teacher"? Why not look to Him? Why not try to find some definite point of contact through our faith and feeling, that we may discover what He really wants us to do. It is not a thing that is impractical, my friends, but we make it so through our doubt, through our constant critical attitude. Oh, how we drive God away from us! and yet we say "We need Thee every hour." We sing hymns and talk glibly of many wonderful things, but when the test comes we fail to apply them. No wonder we lose our faith in the Divine, and the world loses faith in itself.

Epictetus, the great Roman philosopher once wrote: "Have I ever been restrained from what I willed? Or compelled against my will? Indeed how is this possible? I have ranged my pursuits under the direction of God. Is it His Will that I should have a fever? It is my will too. Is it His Will that I should pursue anything? It is my will too. Is it His Will that I should obtain anything? It is my will too. Is it His Will that I should be tortured? Then it is my will to be tortured. Is it His Will that I should die? Then it is my will to die."

What we need is the living example, and more than the living example, we ourselves need to do some of these things. We can do them, but never can they be done through pretense. So long as we think we are cleverer than God, we shall never submit ourselves to His Will no matter how many religious precepts are imposed on us, whether from classical writings, Christian Bible or Buddhist scripture.

Let a man cleanse his heart from egotism! What is

this ego which man asserts every day as he clashes with his fellows? There would be no war in this world, there would be no conflict in our social life or in any phase of our life, were it not for the prevalence of this colossal egotistic tendency in man, which has been increased by his wrong, detrimental training. Man wants everything for himself, and in his blindness even grasps for those things which bring disaster and death. It is not that religion has been at fault, but that we have failed to live our religion. What avails it to say in our prayer, "Thy Will be done!" when all the time we know what we want, and we want God to want that for us? At once there is a division within, and wherever there is division there is lack of strength. If today we are weak spiritually, it is because we have weakened ourselves. And if we ever find our strength, we shall find it through the power of surrender.

There is no word that can convey the grandeur, the beauty, the practical value of this theme of surrender, and I think the moment is ripe for us to draw closer to this great principle. In its light we can even stand up and say: Blessed be the suffering, blessed be the disappointment, blessed be all manner of things that bring us to the consciousness that there is a Higher Power, and that we have been following a mirage, which promises much, but gives absolutely nothing, because it is nothing.

It is not for the weak, this attitude, and by "weak" I do not mean the physically weak, but those who have moral and spiritual weakness. When you see everything crumble before you and yet can rise up and say "I will not interfere with Divine Will," that requires a tremendous amount of strength.

O my friends, this is a very difficult thing to convey
to anyone. Our doubts will arise, confusion will arise
until we have gained a definite concept of what God
is, what Truth is, and of our share in God and in Truth.
A man becomes a giant spiritually when he has given
up all self-seeking. But how can we do this so long
as there is any misgiving in our heart? Let us cultivate
some of these "old-fashioned" ideas, since it seems that
the new-fashioned ideas have not worked out so well.
Try putting into practice the things which you have
accepted theoretically and which you have called your
faith; such, for instance, as "Thy Will be done." It is a
teaching that is accepted by everyone. If you are a Jew
you will say, "Why, we have that in our classics." The
Christian will at once reply, "That is Christ's saying,"
while the Hindu will remark, "We have known that
from four thousand years back." But it is not a question
of how long we have known it. To feel that we possess
something wonderfully ancient does not in itself bring
us any great amount of blessing. Some of your families
have ancient treasures, Bibles, for instance, that the
grandfathers and the grandmothers have carefully preserved and that the descendants take great pride in. As
a matter of fact, they are kept so securely that each
time they are brought out, they have to be dusted. They
are no longer of any use. Same way it is with the ideals
which man keeps on the shelf: they must be put into
practice; the world needs them so tremendously.

We who are seeking today for the solution of our
human problems are no longer satisfied to have clever
people come and give us theories about them. This
country today does not know whom to believe in, and
so it is with every country. In India I have found the

same condition. Men do not want to hear a lot of political discussion by people who are shrewd and diplomatic. They are seeking those who have real vision, who have become clear channels through which the Divine Power is manifesting. You and I can become clear channels. But it requires of us that we wash our mind, our heart, our thought, ourselves clean of all vanity and selfishness, or to sum it up in one word,—of all egotism. Ego plays havoc. It wants to put itself in the place which belongs to Divinity; to set itself upon the throne where God should rule, within the heart where God should reside. This should not be. It is the cause of all our troubles, just as self-surrender, or the practice of the great, grand spiritual concept, "Thy Will be done!" brings peace untold.

You have seen sometimes a little babe lying in its mother's arms—no cares, no fretting—not anxious, not afraid. Same way it can be with us. We are all children, yet the sad thing is, we think we are so grown-up and so wise; and what is more—we desire to instruct others. But what have we to give to others? The more we think of these things, more silent we become.

Let us cleanse our minds that God's Voice may speak through us; His Will may work through us; His Strength may flow through us! How beautiful are some of the great utterances of the mystic souls: "O Lord, make whatever use of me Thou desirest. Take Thou my mind, my heart!—I know not how to use them—do Thou use them for me!"

Some of you who are so clever may say that this is sentimental, and you may easily think it, for you are thinking in one term and I am speaking in another. Such an ideal, however, is not to make us shallow or artificial, but rather to help us so that we may become staunch, undivided in our own home, united with God and with ourselves.

Let us be united! Let us be so unified, so absolutely affiliated with that Great Power that there is no question in our mind at any time. Then when we say, "O Lord, Thy Will be done!" our words will sound like a great musical note and will be for us like a mighty symphony whose volume fills our entire being and the whole world. Blessed is the man who can do this. He is the strongest among us, though he may seem puny and weak. Placed by the side of a great general, pompous and glorious according to our way of life, he may seem as nothing; yet he is the one who wins, who is victorious, because he is united with that Will, that Wisdom, which is eternal and unchangeable.

COMMONWEALTH OF HUMANITY
By Swami Paramananda

ommonwealth of humanity! Is such a thing possible, or is it only a fancy, a dream, a poetic concept? What does it mean? What does it represent? We find it difficult to establish a commonwealth among one group of people, feeling the same way, in one little country, in a county, or even a township. For no matter how small the community, there is always conflict. How then do we ever dare to conceive of a commonwealth of the whole of mankind? Yet upon its accomplishment rests largely our safety, our happiness and our fulfillment.

My destiny once led me—while on a trip around the world—to address a mixed audience at a lecture in Singapore, that great meeting-place of East and West, and on this occasion, I spoke before Chinese, Japanese, Hindus, Moslems, British and American. Now when people so different come together, is there any way of establishing one platform on which all can meet? And what must that platform be? The answer is—Love! And when I say "Love," I ask you not to pass it by with your mind and take it only at its surface value. Try to understand the significance of it, the intensity of it, the fragrance and the healing power that it contains. In the Bible, and in all Bibles, we are told that Love will con-

185

quer all our ills, and we constantly see its working in our everyday life. Christ has taught us that we must love our enemies. Christians say, "Our religion is so wonderful! In our Bible Christ tells us to love those that hate us. He teaches us the allness of love." Mohammedans make similar claims for their faith, and the Buddhists join in with their voices, saying, "Our great Master taught us that hatred is never conquered by hatred. He sent his *Bhikkhus* with the injunction—"O ye *Bhikkhus*, love your enemies, care for the sick, give all men your service." But so long as men talk of love and exhibit hatred, will anyone be convinced by their words?

Now I am not asking you to begin by loving your enemies, or even the people you do not know. I am asking you to love the people you do know. What is the use of reading all these Scriptures if we never make any practical application of them even among our own family and friends? "I want success! I want happiness! I want health! I want prosperity! I want to be in safety!"— here is the cry of every heart. But there can be no safety, not to speak of happiness or well being, until man learns to place himself within the sphere of safety, in an atmosphere of prayer and meditation, where he can breathe the fragrance and feel the very presence of the Infinite.

"Be perfect as your Father which is in heaven." Do not think that this command is only for a Christ or a Christlike spirit. The great personages have achieved it in order that we may do likewise. Let your love so encircle all things that there is no room left for destructive elements. Let it grow; let it expand, that it may represent the one great faith, the great universal idealism, which is the stamp of all systems of belief, and which we shall ever find whenever we go deep down to the heart of any religion. Its fruition is in practical life, and it is man who makes it living. When we contact one who has this mystic expression in his soul—one, for instance, like St. Francis of Assisi—we feel at once that we are in the presence of the Great Deity. It brings to my mind Lessings's conception, embodied in two characters—one a Christian, and the other a Jew. The Christian says to the Jew, "Why, Nathan, you are just like a Christian!" And the Jew replies, "That which makes you feel that I am a Christian makes me feel that you are a Jew." It is not race or creed, it is the motive, the light, the expression of life which brings this reality right before us.

Would you not like to carry in your heart the consciousness that you are part of God?—that you have no disease, no death, no limitation, no more boundary lines?—that through you a mighty power can flow readily without any obstruction? Would you not like to have the All-wise Spirit reflecting through you? After a moment's thought, you may say, "Yes! But that is impossible for mortals." We hypnotize ourselves thinking thus. We think that many things are impossible. We apparently think that it is impossible for a man to seek first the Kingdom of God. Instead, we feel that *after* he has sought all the goods of the world, then he may feel free to pray for his salvation. Sri Ramakrishna gives a parable in illustration of this: A man stood on the beach, waiting to go into the water after all the waves had subsided. But the breakers kept right on, each one bigger than the one before, and there was no cessation. Same way it is when we wait for this world's activities to cease before seeking to find our peace. One man says, "After I have closed up my business affairs I shall take a rest." Another says, "When my son is married I am going to settle down, and perhaps then I shall think about religion." But after the son is married, he finds that there is a grandson who needs looking after, and so it goes on and we continue to fool ourselves, and there is no end.

I am not saying that a man should neglect his duties or his interests, but I am asking him to remember one supremely important interest—an interest that is more vital than wealth or fame or small intellectual gifts. What do we seek when our mind is confused and we know not what to do? Where do we look when we are in darkness? We look for the light—for the light within— and if we cannot find it within, we go to that place where we think it can be found. For it is light alone that can destroy darkness. Light has no label. It makes no difference wherefrom it shines, whether from the east or from the west, from the north or from the south, it is always light, and it is one light.

Now this same great magnitude we find as a basis for the commonwealth of humanity, and the fundamental thought of Love, so far as I can give it utterance, strikes the same universal chord. As we begin to feel a part of this immensity, we are unable to ask, "Is it from America or from England—from India or Japan—from France or from Germany?" It is from everywhere and from nowhere. It is never absent. It is all-abiding, and as we open ourselves to it, as we understand it, all our differences vanish; all pettiness is forgotten, and all our difficulties roll away.

Think this out for yourself. Perhaps you do not like to think things out for yourself. You may prefer to think as your forefathers have taught you. Your forefathers ate and rested in comfort, but you do not feel that that is sufficing and there is no need for you to eat and look out for yourself. The same argument applies to these greater things. Sometimes you feel as if you understood things better than your ancestors did, and must act for your own interest. If that is so, then take also this responsibility.

Man as a human being, must know why he is here. He must know how to take his place here. You may say, "What are the thoughts of one man in this great universe?" One man can cause war, one man can disturb the whole of humanity, unbelievable as this may seem, and also one man can be the preserver of peace. A selfish, vain person can disrupt an entire household, while another type can be such a beneficent influence that even in the midst of anger or disturbance, his very presence guides and soothes. Even places carry an atmosphere. Some places lift the mind, while others make us feel as if they were haunted. They are haunted—by hate and calculation and the evil thoughts of men. We can, if we will, make this world like a paradise. Each one of us can create a center which will inspire men to live sincerely and happily. Each one of us can provide a little bit of impetus to help forward the spirit of unity, harmony and higher living.

The whole idea really is to give inspiration and to receive it. For only as we have it can we convey it to others. If you have a smile, if you have a glow of sunshine in your soul, you do not need to adopt some special utterance to make the fact known. Christ said, "Let your light so shine before men . . . " That is my idea of religion—the remedy for the disease and destruction of the world. It is not by what we say in words that we help anyone, not by our cleverness and our scheming, but only by what naturally and spontaneously and unconsciously comes out of us. Let us live our life in such a manner that an absolute stranger looking upon us, may say, "I feel something living and glowing in this man or woman!" Instead of dividing our house into hundreds and thousands of parts, so that each one is but a little fragment, let us feel the strength of united love, and strike a chord whose divine music may resound throughout the heart of humanity.

Love is

Love is the stongest thing in the world. Love does not grow on trees. Most of the people in the world hate and To really know when love isnear you you will feel Love in your hartt. to Love you can not tell someone you Love them But you your self must feel Love.

Lori G.
age 7

BIBLIOGRAPHY

The Bible. King James Version.

Bucke, Richard Maurice. *Cosmic Consciousness*. New York: E.P. Dutton, 18th edition, 1956.

Daya, Sister. *The Guru and the Disciple*. Cohasset, Mass.: Vedanta Centre Publishers, 1976.

Devamata, Sister. *Swami Paramananda and His Work*. Cohasset, Mass.: Vedanta Centre Publishers, 1926.

Gleick, James. *Chaos—Making a New Science*. New York: Penguin Books, 1987.

Hixon, Lex. *Great Swan—Meetings with Ramakrishna*. Boston: Shambhala Publications, 1992.

Khan, Hazrat Inayat. *The Music of Life*. New Lebanon, N.Y.: Omega Press, 1983.

Levinsky, Sara Ann. *A Bridge of Dreams—The Story of Swami Paramananda, a Modern Mystic—and His Ideal of All-Conquering Love*. West Stockbridge, Mass.: The Lindesfarne Press, 1984.

Margenau, Henry and Roy Abraham Varghese, eds. *Cosmos, Bios, Theos*. La Salle, IL.: Open Court Press, 1992.

Moyers, Bill. *A World of Ideas II*. New York: Doubleday, 1990.

Newell, Norman D.. *Creation and Evolution*. New York: Columbia University Press, 1982.

Nicolescu, Basarab. *Science, Meaning, and Evolution—The Cosmology of Jacob Boehme.* New York: Parabola Books, 1991.

Nouy, Lecomte du. *Human Destiny.* New York: Longmans, Green and Co., 1947.

Paramananda, Swami. *Reincarnation and Immortality.* Cohasset, Mass.: Vedanta Centre Publishers, 1961; reprint edition.

_____. *Christ and Oriental Ideals.* Cohasset Mass.: Vedanta Centre Publishers, 1968; reprint edition.

_____. *Emerson and Vedanta.* Cohasset, Mass.: Vedanta Centre Publishers, 1918.

_____. *Plato and Vedic Idealism.* Cohasset, Mass.: Vedanta Centre Publishers, 1924.

_____. *Vedanta Monthly, Message of the East,* 1912-1940; 1958, 1961.

Peace Pilgrim. *Peace Pilgrim—Her Life and Work in Her Own Words.* Compiled by some of her friends. Santa Fe: Ocean Tree Books, 1983.

Prabhavananda, Swami. *How to Know God—The Yoga Aphorisms of Patanjali.* Hollywood, CA.: Vedanta Society of Southern California, 1953.

Salk, Jonas. *Anatomy of Reality—Merging of Intuition and Reason.* New York: Columbia University Press, 1983.

Saradananda, Swami. *Sri Ramakrishna—The Great Master.* Madras: Sri Ramakrishna Math, 1952.

Toms, Michael. *At the Leading Edge—New Visions of Science, Spirituality and Society.* Burdett, New York: Larson Publications, 1991.

Vivekananda, Swami. *The Complete Works of Swami Vivekananda.* Vols. I,II,III. Mayavati: Advaita Ashrama, 1976.

_____. *Jnana Yoga.* Calcutta: Advaita Ashrama, 1980.

ABOUT THE AUTHORS

Sri Ramakrishna (1836-1886). "Ramakrishna is not a quaint person from an ancient culture, representing a particular religious background, but an Einstein of the planetary civilization of the future evolution of humanity."

Lex Hixon in *Great Swan*

Vivekananda (1863-1902). Foremost disciple of Sri Ramakrishna; first swami to teach in America; guru of Paramananda.

Swami Saradananda (1865-1927). Direct disciple of Sri Ramakrishna; lectured in America from 1896 until 1898; author of the most authoritative biography of Sri Ramakrishna, *Sri Ramakrishna, The Great Master.*

Swami Ramakrishnananda (1863-1911). Direct disciple of Sri Ramakrishna; founder of the Madras Math; mentor of Paramananda.

Swami Paramananda (1884-1940). Outstanding disciple of Vivekananda; spiritual teacher, mystic, philosopher, author, poet; conducted thirty-four years of ministry in the United States and lectured all over the world.

Sister Devamata (1867-1942). Introduced to Vedanta by Swami Vivekananda in 1899 and editor of many of his works. Sister Devamata was Paramananda's first disciple and first platform assistant; author of *Paramananda and His Work (Two Volumes).*

Sister Daya (1882-1955). Poet, playwright, author of *The Guru and the Disciple*, about her life as a diciple of Paramananda. She became his platform assistant.

ACKNOWLEDGMENT

Grateful acknowledgment to the following for permission to use quotations from their copyrighted publications:

Advaita Ashrama, Mayavati, India
G.P. Putnam, New York
Sri Ramakrishna Math, Madras, India
Vedanta Press, Hollywood, CA.
The Vedanta Centre Publishers,
 Cohasset, MA.
La Crescenta, CA.

My special gratitude to Srimata Gayatri Devi for her loving permission and support of our project; to Dr. Jonas Salk for the first inspiration for our title; to Rina Dion, our designer, who always brings love and enthusiasm to her work; and to others, unnamed, who contributed inestimable help, adding love and joy in the doing.

But most of all, my deepest gratitude to my Friend for His unfailing Strength and constant Guidance. As Swami Paramananda says, "Thank God for everything!" God is the Doer. Not I.

April 17, 1993